INTRODUCING
ISSUES WITH
OPPOSING
VIEWPOINTS®

Banned Books

Cynthia A. Bily, *Book Editor*

GREENHAVEN PRESS
A part of Gale, Cengage Learning

GALE
CENGAGE Learning·

Detroit • New York • San Francisco • New Haven, Conn • Waterville, Maine • London

Elizabeth Des Chenes, *Managing Editor*

For more information, contact:
Greenhaven Press
27500 Drake Rd.
Farmington Hills, MI 48331-3535
Or you can visit our Internet site at gale.cengage.com

For product information and technology assistance, contact us at

Gale Customer Support, 1-800-877-4253
For permission to use material from this text or product, submit all requests online at www.cengage.com/permissions

Further permissions questions can be e-mailed to permissionrequest@cengage.com

Articles in Greenhaven Press anthologies are often edited for length to meet page requirements. In addition, original titles of these works are changed to clearly present the main thesis and to explicitly indicate the author's opinion. Every effort is made to ensure that Greenhaven Press accurately reflects the original intent of the authors. Every effort has been made to trace the owners of copyrighted material.

Cover image © Steve Skjold/Alamy.

LIBRARY OF CONGRESS CATALOGING-IN-PUBLICATION DATA

Banned books / Cynthia A. Bily, book editor.
    p. cm. -- (Introducing issues with opposing viewpoints)
  Summary: "Banned Books: Should Children Be Protected from Controversial Books?; Should Certain Kinds of Material Be Restricted?; What Are Some Alternatives to Banning Controversial Books?"-- Provided by publisher.
  Includes bibliographical references and index.
  ISBN 978-0-7377-5671-5
  1. Censorship--Juvenile literature. 2. Challenged books--Juvenile literature. 3. Prohibited books--Juvenile literature. 4. Libraries--Censorship--Juvenile literature. 5. Children--Books and reading--Juvenile literature. I. Bily, Cynthia A.
  Z657.B195 2012
  363.31--dc23

                                         2011036231

Printed in the United States of America
1 2 3 4 5 6 7 16 15 14 13 12

Contents

Chapter 3: What Are Some Alternatives to Banning Controversial Books?

Foreword

Indulging in a wide spectrum of ideas, beliefs, and perspectives is a critical cornerstone of democracy. After all, it is often debates over differences of opinion, such as whether to legalize abortion, how to treat prisoners, or when to enact the death penalty, that shape our society and drive it forward. Such diversity of thought is frequently regarded as the hallmark of a healthy and civilized culture. As the Reverend Clifford Schutjer of the First Congregational Church in Mansfield, Ohio, declared in a 2001 sermon, "Surrounding oneself with only like-minded people, restricting what we listen to or read only to what we find agreeable is irresponsible. Refusing to entertain doubts once we make up our minds is a subtle but deadly form of arrogance." With this advice in mind, Introducing Issues with Opposing Viewpoints books aim to open readers' minds to the critically divergent views that comprise our world's most important debates.

Introducing Issues with Opposing Viewpoints simplifies for students the enormous and often overwhelming mass of material now available via print and electronic media. Collected in every volume is an array of opinions that captures the essence of a particular controversy or topic. Introducing Issues with Opposing Viewpoints books embody the spirit of nineteenth-century journalist Charles A. Dana's axiom: "Fight for your opinions, but do not believe that they contain the whole truth, or the only truth." Absorbing such contrasting opinions teaches students to analyze the strength of an argument and compare it to its opposition. From this process readers can inform and strengthen their own opinions, or be exposed to new information that will change their minds. Introducing Issues with Opposing Viewpoints is a mosaic of different voices. The authors are statesmen, pundits, academics, journalists, corporations, and ordinary people who have felt compelled to share their experiences and ideas in a public forum. Their words have been collected from newspapers, journals, books, speeches, interviews, and the Internet, the fastest growing body of opinionated material in the world.

Introducing Issues with Opposing Viewpoints shares many of the well-known features of its critically acclaimed parent series, Opposing Viewpoints. The articles are presented in a pro/con format, allowing readers to absorb divergent perspectives side by side. Active reading questions preface each viewpoint, requiring the student to approach the material thoughtfully and carefully. Useful charts, graphs, and cartoons supplement each article. A thorough introduction provides readers with crucial background on an issue. An annotated bibliography points the reader toward articles, books, and websites that contain additional information on the topic. An appendix of organizations to contact contains a wide variety of charities, nonprofit organizations, political groups, and private enterprises that each hold a position on the issue at hand. Finally, a comprehensive index allows readers to locate content quickly and efficiently.

Introducing Issues with Opposing Viewpoints is also significantly different from Opposing Viewpoints. As the series title implies, its presentation will help introduce students to the concept of opposing viewpoints and learn to use this material to aid in critical writing and debate. The series' four-color, accessible format makes the books attractive and inviting to readers of all levels. In addition, each viewpoint has been carefully edited to maximize a reader's understanding of the content. Short but thorough viewpoints capture the essence of an argument. A substantial, thought-provoking essay question placed at the end of each viewpoint asks the student to further investigate the issues raised in the viewpoint, compare and contrast two authors' arguments, or consider how one might go about forming an opinion on the topic at hand. Each viewpoint contains sidebars that include at-a-glance information and handy statistics. A Facts About section located in the back of the book further supplies students with relevant facts and figures.

Following in the tradition of the Opposing Viewpoints series, Greenhaven Press continues to provide readers with invaluable exposure to the controversial issues that shape our world. As John Stuart Mill once wrote: "The only way in which a human being can make some approach to knowing the whole of a subject is by hearing what can be said about it by persons of every variety of opinion and studying all modes in which it can be looked at by every character of mind. No wise man ever acquired his wisdom in any mode but this." It is to this principle that Introducing Issues with Opposing Viewpoints books are dedicated.

Introduction

"Books usually are challenged with the best intentions—to protect others, frequently children, from difficult ideas and information."

—American Library Association, "About Banned and Challenged Books," www.ala.org.

Native American author Sherman Alexie's first young-adult novel, *The Absolutely True Diary of a Part-Time Indian* (2007), won nearly every important award a young-adult novel can win, including the National Book Award for Young People's Literature, the *Boston Globe*–Horn Book Award for Excellence in Children's Literature in Fiction, even Sweden's Peter Pan Award. Reviewers widely praised the book: *Minneapolis Star Tribune* reviewer Jim Lenfestey called the novel a "very funny bright light among the lost"; Teenreads.com writer Jana Siciliano called it "an uplifting yet very emotional reading experience"; and *New York Times* reviewer Bruce Barcott called it "a gem of a book." High schools across the country quickly embraced the novel, adding it to Advanced Placement courses, summer reading lists, and school libraries.

But not everyone felt so positively about the book, which describes a poor fourteen-year-old Native American boy's first year in a wealthy all-white high school. Many parents were troubled by the book's language and by its references to alcohol and masturbation. In a 2009 story in the *Chicago Tribune*, reporter Ruth Fuller described some parents' reactions after the book was assigned as summer reading by Antioch High School in a Chicago suburb. "I can't imagine anyone finding this book appropriate for a 13- or 14-year-old," said the mother of a 14-year-old boy. "This is not appropriate for our community." Parents at Antioch demanded the book be removed from the curriculum and the library. In Stockton, Missouri, the Stockton R-l School Board agreed unanimously to keep the book out of the local high school after parents complained in September 2010. According to a story by Adam Stillman, writing for the website CedarRepublican.com, handouts at the board meeting enumerated seventy-four instances of "vulgarity" in the novel, and board member Ken Spurgeon declared, "We can take this book and we can wrap it in those 20 awards everybody said it won, and you know what, it is still wrong." After winning several regional, national, and international awards in 2007 and 2008, *The Absolutely True Diary of a Part-Time Indian* became, according to records kept by the American Library Association (ALA), the second-most challenged book of 2010.

A book challenge, as defined by the ALA, is "an attempt to remove or restrict materials, based upon the objections of a person or group. A banning is the removal of those materials." True book banning is rare in the United States (the last time the federal government prohibited a book from being imported or sold in this country was 1963), but smaller groups, including schools or school districts, may decide that a book may not be taught in class or borrowed from a library or that it must be restricted to adult readers.

Several reviewers of *The Absolutely True Diary* praised the book for its insightful handling of alcoholism and the harm it has brought to Native Americans; many parents believe that teens should not be reading about alcoholism or other sad or harsh parts of life or that books about Native Americans and alcohol reinforce negative stereotypes. While reviewers admired Alexie's ability to capture the way fourteen-year-old boys talk, including their use of vulgar language, many parents argued that children should not be exposed to vulgar language. The American Library Association reports that the novel has been challenged because of "offensive language, racism, sex education, sexually explicit, unsuited to age group, and violence."

People disagree about why these and other book challenges—most of which are brought by parents—occur. Well-known children's author Judy Blume speaks for many when she writes on her website, "I believe that censorship grows out of fear, and because fear is contagious, some parents are easily swayed. . . . They want to believe that if their children don't read about it, their children won't know about it. And if they don't know about it, it won't happen." But many parents believe that students should learn about controversial topics from their parents, not at school or in the library. As John Davis, a Virginia father quoted in a 2009 FoxNews.com story, put it, "Teachers are supposed to be teaching our kids what they need to know educationally. These kinds of things are the parent's responsibility."

Book challenges come from all kinds of people with all kinds of beliefs. Some Christians might object to books that teach the theory of evolution or to books like the Harry Potter series that describe witchcraft in a positive light, while believers of other faiths—or those with no faith—might object to the Bible being used in public schools. Challenges have been raised to books that encourage traditional views that some see as racist or sexist and also to books encouraging newer views like support for homosexuality or environmentalism. In almost every case, as the quotation that opens this introduction affirms, the challengers have good intentions. As people of good will work to determine the best ways to balance intellectual freedom with responsible adulthood, they must struggle with three important questions: Should children be protected from controversial books? Should certain kinds of material be restricted? What are some alternatives to banning controversial books? The authors of the following viewpoints present a range of answers to these questions.

Chapter 1

Should Children Be Protected from Controversial Books?

The public library in Gadsden, Alabama, presents a banned books display. The American Library Association encourages readers not to judge books by their covers—but without them.

School Libraries and Curricula Should Not Focus on Books That Include Violence and Pornography

"The idea that our Founding Fathers wrote the First Amendment to allow children to view obscene literature is preposterous."

Steve Baldwin

In the following viewpoint Steve Baldwin argues that a wave of new literature, called "authentic literature," poses a threat to children. These books, featuring druggies, gang members, and other characters on the fringes of society, have increasingly become introduced to public school libraries over the past few years. Although proponents of the genre claim these books portray American life in a more realistic fashion, Baldwin argues that these selections contain offensive material, such as violence and pornography, and should not be assigned

Steve Baldwin, "Parents Protest American Library Association's 'Censorship,'" *Human Events,* January 17, 2006. www.humanevents.com. Copyright © 2006 *Human Events.* All rights reserved. Reproduced by permission.

as mandatory reading. Books containing obscenities undermine America's value system, Baldwin concludes, and should not be available at public schools.

Steve Baldwin is the executive director of the Council for National Policy. He previously served as a state legislator in California where he chaired the Assembly Education Committee.

AS YOU READ, CONSIDER THE FOLLOWING QUESTIONS:
1. How does Baldwin define "authentic literature"?
2. How does the author support his argument that ALA's claims of being "First Amendment guardians . . . look fraudulent"?
3. What are two books that Baldwin lists as examples of obscene literature?

C ontroversies over books in public libraries—mostly school libraries—have been around for decades but a new round of protests by parents is breaking out in Maryland, Virginia, California, Arkansas and other states.

With the introduction of a new genre of literature and the presence of the Internet, this battle has taken some new twists. Moreover, much of the usual propaganda promulgated by the American Library Association (ALA) regarding "censorship" and "book burning" is increasingly falling on deaf ears.

> ## Fast Fact
>
> The Citizens for Literary Standards in Schools website lists thirty books containing the "f-word" that have been approved, assigned, or promoted in local high schools.

It's a dirty little secret that the librarians of today are far removed from the prim and proper characterization which for years was part of American lore; today, these professionals—more precisely, the ALA—has taken its place among the militant left and has staked out positions well beyond the mainstream.

There are very few libraries today in which I would leave my 13-year-old son unescorted, because, unfortunately, the protection and safety of our children is simply no longer a priority for libraries or for the ALA. That may sound harsh, but it's true and the shrill cry of censorship one constantly hears emanating from the ALA is really disturbing considering the shocking books they defend.

"Authentic Literature"

Unbeknownst to most people, a new wave of literature called "authentic literature" hit our public school libraries over the last few years. The ALA claims such books portray American life and culture in a

The author deplores the new wave of "authentic literature" now found in school libraries. He argues that such material is not "realistic"—as the American Library Association claims— but is peppered with unsavory characters and situations.

more realistic fashion. But they don't. These books feature druggies, sex addicts, pedophiles, gang members and others on the fringes of society. Increasingly, this literature is replacing the traditional literature classics, which, in general, promoted mainstream American values or at least didn't undermine them.

The authentic literature books are rife with profanity and are dominated by themes of death, crime, drug addiction, rapes, gang beatings, weird sex, homosexual encounters, and so on. Shockingly, many of them violate state obscenity laws and even school district age appropriate regulations. In my former capacity as Chairman of the California Legislature's Education Committee, I collected excerpts from hundreds of such books that are not only common in school libraries but are often assigned by teachers as mandatory reading assignments.

Naturally, parent groups have formed to protest such books and many have put up websites with excerpts, but much of it is too graphic for me to repeat here. The best of the parent web sites is www.pabbis.com; take a look and weep. Yes, this is the trash many of our public schools are feeding America's youth. The books that used to inspire; which celebrated American values; that chronicled the exploits of trailblazers, astronauts, soldiers, and other heroes, are fast disappearing. And their replacements are books like: *A Woman in Heat Wiping Herself, Outside the Operating Room of a Sex-Change Doctor*, and the *Rainbow Boys*, a story of three homosexual boys and the various routes they took in "coming out."

The ALA response to parental complaints was the creation a few years ago of a national event they call "Banned Books Week" in which outrageous charges are made about parents supposedly attempting to ban classics like *Huckleberry Finn* and *Of Mice and Men*. It's an ingenious tactic considering the ALA seems intent on phasing out the classics. However, parent researchers and bloggers have found many of these allegations to be false or grossly exaggerated; for example, the ALA counts as censorship incidents in which a parent simply requests that the school or library be more age selective when assigning books or amend a teacher's mandatory reading list to include other books not so offensive.

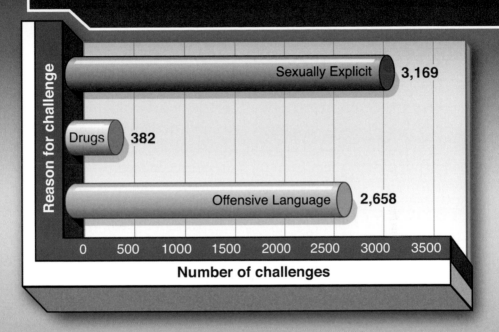

Challenged Books, 1990–2010

Thousands of attempts, for a variety of reasons, were made to have books removed from schools and libraries from 1990 to 2010, according to the American Library Association.

Reason for challenge

Sexually Explicit — 3,169

Drugs — 382

Offensive Language — 2,658

0   500   1000   1500   2000   2500   3000   3500

Number of challenges

Taken from: American Library Association, 2011.

For making the modest demand that schools not flood their children's minds with filth until, for example, the 8th grade, the ALA, PTA, various state Department of Educations and some loony anti-Christian groups have responded by publishing outlandish strategy manuals on how to deal with "extremists," the code word for any parent with a religious-based value system.

The ALA and the First Amendment

But the ALA will not compromise on such common-sense requests by parents. Banned Books Week was clearly designed by the ALA to direct attention away from the onslaught of violent, obscene literature in America's schools. And it's not just books; it's the Internet as well. When I co-sponsored a bill to have filters placed on library computers so as to block pornographic and racist web sites, the ALA went ballistic. They flew in their big guns and in front of a hearing room full of shocked parents, argued that "the First Amendment is more important than parental concerns about content" and made clear they were totally against any effort to block content of any kind from children no matter what age. Indeed, the ALA web site arrogantly states, "Librarians do not serve in loco parentis [in the place of a parent]."

The idea that our Founding Fathers wrote the First Amendment to allow children to view obscene literature is preposterous but the ALA is on a crusade to persuade all libraries to treat children as adults. It's a bizarre crusade, because, legally and morally, school children are minors and school boards and librarians have been entrusted by parents to protect them from such literature. Indeed, when a library Internet filter bill was introduced in Congress, the ALA went all out to fight it. It passed but ended up in the courts where again, the ALA spent a fortune fighting it all the way to the U.S. Supreme Court. They lost. Thank God.

A 2000 report by the Family Research Council details how its researchers sent out surveys to every librarian in America asking questions about access to pornography. Despite efforts by the ALA to stop its members from responding, 462 librarians did respond. Their replies revealed 472 instances of children accessing pornography, 962 instances of adults accessing pornography, 106 instances of adults exposing children to pornography, five attempted child molestations, 144 instances of child porn being accessed and 25 instances of library staff being harassed by those viewing pornography. Over 2,062 total porn-related incidents were reported by a mere 4.6% of our nation's librarians so one can assume the number of incidents is probably twenty times higher.

One would think after a Supreme Court loss and the increasing danger of perverts and pedophiles creeping about libraries, the ALA would shift to more important issues, like helping children learn how to read, but no, the battle promptly shifted back to literature. Indeed, one can make a case that since their hands are now tied regarding Internet porn, ALA members have intensified their efforts to purchase highly inappropriate literature.

Undermining American Values

The ALA's bias is so obvious that when parent groups have offered to place books in libraries with conservative themes or are critical of the left, the ALA's claims of being First Amendment guardians suddenly look fraudulent. When one parent tried to donate George Grant's book, *Killer Angel,* a critical biography of Planned Parenthood founder Margaret Sanger, the library sent a letter stating that "the author's political and social agenda . . . is not appropriate." Huh? A biographical book with zero profanity is banned but books that feature the "F" word a hundred times are sought after with zeal. Go figure.

Ironically, the biggest censor in America today is currently the ALA. Libraries with limited budgets make decisions every day as to which books to purchase or not to purchase. Such decisions are often based on recommendations from the ALA. With hundreds of thousands of libraries in America today, the purposeful actions of librarians to not select books with a conservative perspective is having an enormous impact on our culture, our value system and our youth. Remember, most teachers get their ideas for student reading assignments from the school library and the ALA targets classroom teachers with press releases promoting certain books.

Nowhere is the ALA's bias more obvious than issues regarding homosexuality. The ALA's huge Gay, Lesbian, Bisexual, and Transgendered Round Table works closely with many of the nation's gay activist groups to place into libraries books glorifying the homosexual lifestyle. As a result, one will often find the ratio of pro-homosexual books to books critical of the gay agenda massively in favor of the former. Books by ex-gays are nearly impossible to find. Among the numerous pro-gay workshops at ALA's annual convention are Building and Promoting GLBT (Gay, Lesbian, Bisexual, [and] Transgendered) Children's and Young Adult Collections. The homosexual books most heavily promoted by the ALA are those which receive its "Stonewall Award" like, *At Swim, Two Boys,* and *Lawnboy,* both replete with pedophilia themes. Nor is it uncommon to find in today's libraries graphic homosexual newspapers rife with obscene personal ads.

It has become increasingly clear that the ALA is really not so much dedicated to defending the First Amendment as it is to challenging

America's underlying value system. It's time to acknowledge that libraries have changed. Those who think their children are safe in libraries today need to know that many of our libraries have been transformed from the caretakers of knowledge to key players in the militant movement to undermine America's Judeo-Christian heritage.

EVALUATING THE AUTHOR'S ARGUMENTS:

The author of this viewpoint, Steve Baldwin, is the parent of a thirteen-year-old son. As a parent, Baldwin seems primarily to address other parents in his call to remove obscene material from school libraries. How might the viewpoint be revised if it were intended to be read by teachers? Or students? What changes in language, in tone and in content would the author make to appeal effectively to these other audiences?

Schools Are the Ideal Place for Controversial Topics to Be Addressed

National Coalition Against Censorship

"School . . . can provide a place for young people to explore difficult issues safely."

The following viewpoint, from the National Coalition Against Censorship (NCAC), argues that it is part of the public schools' responsibility to teach democratic values of fairness, equality, and respect and that an important part of meeting this responsibility is exposing students to a wide range of beliefs and ideas. Families have differing ideas about subjects like sex, race, and religion, the author acknowledges, but no one parent or group of parents should be allowed to determine what all children learn about just because the ideas of others conflict with their own. In fact, the NCAC concludes, school is an ideal place for students to gain exposure to others' viewpoints, because a classroom discussion will be led by an experienced teacher and conducted with civility.

The National Coalition against Censorship is an alliance of literary, artistic, religious, educational, and professional groups opposed to all forms of censorship.

AS YOU READ, CONSIDER THE FOLLOWING QUESTIONS:
1. According to the author, a shared commitment to what can provide a common ground for resolving differences?
2. Which two topics are most likely to generate tension and debate, as reported by the NCAC?
3. Why, according to the author, do some people believe that discussing profanity in the classroom could teach valuable lessons?

Adherence to democratic values and a commitment to the Constitution create a common culture out of the many ethnic, religious, and racial groups that comprise this land of immigrant and native Americans. Ethnic pride and differing individual beliefs flourish in America, because we recognize that they are all part of our common culture. Respect for cultural pluralism is at the core of American democracy.

The democratic values taught in public schools complement the social and religious values taught in the home and in the church, temple, synagogue, or mosque. Students learn to understand and articulate the values they have learned at home by participating in classroom assignments and discussions where they are free to study a variety of information and differing views about an issue and to express their own opinions.

When parents and educators disagree on an issue that touches on social and religious values, a shared commitment to essential democratic values can provide the common ground for resolving differences of opinion. Fairness and justice require that no one parent's view should prevail over all others. Freedom allows parents to express their particular concerns and seek an accommodation to address them. Respect for others dictates that any conflict be resolved with civility.

Teachers and school officials need to be sensitive to parents' concerns and to the many different styles of parenting, and parents likewise must be cognizant of the responsibility of teachers to exercise their professional judgment to choose educationally suitable materials for all students.

Learning About Life—Safely

Young people mature into healthy, responsible adults by acquiring basic skills and information and by learning from trustworthy adults how to address real issues that arise in their homes, communities, and workplaces.

Students, like teachers and parents, face complex, difficult problems every day, and they learn about societal problems from newspapers and television. They bring their questions and experiences to school, which can provide a place for young people to explore difficult issues safely.

Educators respond to the wide range of students' concerns with information suited to their needs and stage of development. This is a critical function of schools, one that complements students' basic education in meaningful ways.

Educators continually wrestle with a dilemma: whether to address the questions and concerns students raise, or to avoid difficult issues for fear of offending a few. Although most try to be sensitive to the beliefs and feelings of students and their parents, teachers would be abdicating their responsibilities, and perhaps short-changing those who need their help, if they decided to solve this continuing dilemma by simply ignoring the difficult issues.

> **FAST FACT**
>
> Thirty-five states, as well as the District of Columbia, allow parents to keep their children out of school sex education classes, according to the National Conference of State Legislatures.

Life can be difficult and contentious, because people disagree strongly about some of the most important issues. That's the reality. Schools are like laboratories where students can learn and practice the skills they will need in life.

The National Coalition Against Censorship (NCAC) holds a forum on school censorship. The NCAC argues that that exposing students to controversial topics teaches them tolerance and respect for different cultures.

Why Educators Teach Controversial Topics

In order to provide a well-rounded and relevant education, teachers sometimes use materials that some people find controversial. Materials used in school to address sexuality and religion, or to deal with race or ethnicity, have stimulated controversy and calls for censorship because these are sensitive subjects. Like parents, teachers are increasingly called upon to address such issues in response to events in the news or inquiries from students. Good teachers will seize the "teachable moment" and make use of such controversial topics to help students develop critical thinking skills. Often videos and literary selections can be effective tools in such discussions.

Materials discussing sex and religion are particularly likely to generate tension and debate.

Caring adults are understandably concerned about teenagers' decisions and behavior regarding sex, and educators respect the right of parents to teach their children their own rules and values governing sexual relationships. Since many teenagers are sexually active, however, and some parents do not provide adequate information to their children, the school must assume an increasingly important role in providing such information. Most health educators feel an obligation to provide their students with factual information about sexuality to help them make informed decisions. Moreover, most parents approve of sex education that includes a professionally developed curriculum containing scientific and health-related information. In most districts, those parents who prefer that their child not have such information are allowed to opt out of sex education.

Religion also sparks controversies, as some parents object to the teaching of any ideas that differ from their religious beliefs. These can include beliefs about sexuality, the role of women, biology, history, or other topics. Educators must respect the religious beliefs of all students and cannot make curricular decisions catering to any one religion, or even the majority's religious preferences. As a result, conflict sometimes arises over the tension between parents' desires that their own religious beliefs take precedence and the educators' need to be neutral. By teaching tolerance and respect for the rich religious diversity of this country, schools reaffirm each child's own religion or non-belief while strengthening America as a nation of many religions.

In recent years, some parents have denounced classic works of literature that use racial epithets or profanity because they fear the books will increase racial animosity and harm their children. Others think such books can be used to increase understanding of the evils of prejudice, or weaken the appeal of profanity by exposing it to serious discussion in the classroom. These works can teach valuable lessons and help students appreciate social rules and expectations.

Students Benefit from Learning About Controversies

The classroom is a good place to learn about controversial and offensive ideas. There, students have the benefit of a teacher to guide their discussion and help them conduct that discussion with respect and civility. In the safe space of the classroom, younger students can learn the excitement of reading such books as *The Great Gilly Hopkins, Scary Stories to Tell in the Dark*, or the works of Roald Dahl. Through teachers, older students can appreciate both historical context and

Religious Affiliation in the United States

Families in the United States practice a wide variety of religions. The largest groups, as reported in a survey of more than 35,000 adults conducted in 2007 by the Pew Forum on Religion and Public Life, are shown here.

Religious Affiliation	Percentage
Evangelical Protestant churches	26.3
Catholic	23.9
Mainline Protestant churches	18.1
Unaffiliated	16.1
Historically black churches	6.9
Mormon	1.7
Jewish	1.7
Other faiths	1.2
Don't know/refused	0.8
Jehovah's Witness	0.7
Buddhist	0.7
Orthodox	0.6
Muslim	0.6
Hindu	0.4
Other Christian	0.3
Other world religions	<0.3

Taken from: Pew Forum on Religion & Public Life, US Religious Landscape Survey, May 8 to August 13, 2007.

the many layers of meaning in literature such as *The Adventures of Huckleberry Finn, The Merchant of Venice,* or *Of Mice and Men.* Students would miss out on more than history if these kinds of materials were omitted from the classroom.

EVALUATING THE AUTHOR'S ARGUMENTS:

The first two viewpoints in this book are very different in tone. In the previous viewpoint, Steve Baldwin describes his outrage over a new wave of books containing objectionable material that are now found in schools and libraries. This viewpoint, from the National Coalition Against Censorship, maintains a calm, unemotional tone and gives few specific details. Which approach do you find more convincing? What reasons might these specific authors have for adopting these specific voices?

Parents Should Work to Restrict What Schools and Libraries Present to Children

Erin Manning

> "Even if [objectionable] works rose to great literary heights parents would not be out of line to ask that they be moved from the middle school library."

In the viewpoint that follows, Erin Manning argues that parents have a responsibility to know what school libraries contain and to ask that inappropriate books be removed. It is no longer the case, she contends, that parents can rely on teachers and librarians to make good decisions about what materials are suitable; too many of them, she explains, do not have the same moral standards as parents. Because libraries have a record of giving children books with depictions of sex and violence, she concludes, parents must reclaim the responsibility for deciding what books are available to children.

Manning, a writer who labels herself a "homeschooling mom," writes a blog called *And Sometimes Tea*, addressed to Roman Catholic readers.

AS YOU READ, CONSIDER THE FOLLOWING QUESTIONS:
1. As defined by the author, what is a "challenge" to a book?
2. Which novel briefly described by Manning is written in "chat speak"?
3. What does the author say motivates publishers to produce so many "lousy, substandard, second-rate" books?

D uring the last week of September every year, the American Library Association [ALA] holds what it calls "Banned Book Week." The purpose of this week, the ALA says, is to highlight "the benefits of free and open access to information while drawing attention to the harms of censorship by spotlighting actual or attempted bannings of books across the United States."

It sounds like a noble endeavour, right? In this day and age I think it would be hard to find people who would actively support the notion of outright censorship. Yet we know that at other times and in different kinds of regimes around the world this dedication to free speech has not always been the rule. Keeping the principle of free speech safe requires vigilance; if people in America really were seeking to ban books—to forbid their printing or sale, for instance—it would be important to focus on their efforts and to raise awareness about them.

But that kind of "banning" isn't what the ALA is talking about at all.

Not Banning, but Parenting

In fact, according to their website, the ALA's Banned Book Week is really called "Banned and Challenged Book Week." A "challenge" to a book occurs when someone objects to some of the content of a book, and, most of the time, asks that the book be removed from children's access. Parents were responsible for 57% of such challenges between 1990 and 2008, and an astonishing 70% of the challenges involved books that were either in a school classroom or a school library. Moreover, nearly a third of challenges made to all books (including books aimed at adults) were made because the challengers found the materials to be too sexually explicit.

Now, if the vast majority of challenges to books involve parents, centre around books available in schools, and deal with such issues as sexual explicitness, offensive language, or the unsuitability of the books for a specific age group, then I think we're no longer talking about book-banning or censorship. I think we're talking about parenting.

The attitude of the ALA is that a parent only has the right to censor or control what his own children read. He doesn't have the right to request the removal from the school library or classroom shelf those books which he finds obscene or dangerous to morality, because someone else might prefer for his children to read those books. The school alone has the final say in what books are appropriate for the children under its care to read, and if a child reads at school a book or books which his parents absolutely forbid at home—well, then, perhaps the parents' values are too narrow and restrictive to begin with.

Schools and Libraries Cannot Be Trusted

Here's the dilemma for parents, though—there was a time when we could trust schools and libraries to support, for the most part, the same values we ourselves held, and to abide by community standards of morality and decency. There was a time when it would have been just as unthinkable to the librarian or the school teacher as to a parent that a book for children would have contained the following things:

- Graphic language about sex, drinking, drugs; laced with profanity and written in "chat speak" (*TTYL* by Lauren Myracle)
- Violence, implied sex, anti-religious and anti-Christian messages throughout; God is literally killed (*His Dark Materials* by Philip Pullman)
- Prostitution, witchcraft, voodoo, devil worship (*Bless Me, Ultima* by Rudolfo Anaya)
- Homosexuality, drugs, suicide, sex, nudity (*The Perks of Being a Wallflower* by Stephen Chbosky)
- Sex, drugs, alcohol, eating disorders, profanity, smoking (*Gossip Girl* series by Cecily von Ziegesar)

These are some of the objectionable content found in just five of the ten most frequently challenged books for 2008. Given that most

The Gossip Girl *series has caused some librarians and parent groups to call for the books to be banned because of the author's depictions of teen involvement in such activities as sex, drugs, and alcohol.*

challengers are parents and most challenges involve books in school libraries or school classrooms, I'd be much more worried about society if books like these were never questioned at all.

Many of the challenges to these books are due to their presence on middle school bookshelves (or even in class assignments); middle school students can be as young as eleven years old. And yet the ALA views parental challenges to these books as being somehow akin to book-burnings and government censorship, as if there were no legitimate reason why a group of parents might not want their children reading novels in which gratuitous and explicit sex, violence, drug use, and the like were major elements of the story.

Mindless, Substandard Books

The fact is, there are plenty of good reasons to object to books with these content elements in them, especially when such young children are the ones who have access to these books. Even if the works rose to great literary heights parents would not be out of line to ask that they be moved from the middle school library; but most of these books are not, frankly, works of much merit at all. They are the fiction equivalent of mindless TV programs, complete with pandering, fantasy, commercialised writing, and shock value in place of decent storytelling, a well-developed plot, interesting and three-dimensional characters, and some idea of consequences for actions.

FAST FACT

Since the first Banned Books Week in 1982, more than one thousand books have been banned or challenged.

To put it bluntly, the ALA puts itself in the position of defending lousy, substandard, second-rate writing that would probably not even be published in the first place, were it not for the insatiable appetite for inappropriate content usually euphemised as "dark" or "edgy" by the sort of pre-teen who thinks angsty, brooding, sparkly vampires are a good idea. And they cast parents in the role of villains, as if their well-founded concerns about the content and merit of these books were on a par with Nazi book-burning efforts.

Parents Must Be More Vigilant than Ever

It is clear that in many instances the library and the school, as political entities, no longer share the cultural values of the vast majority of parents. We are living through a time of cultural divide—and whether you think it's a good or a terrible idea for novels aimed at eleven-year-olds to contain sex and violence is largely going to depend on which side of that divide you and your family is on.

Because we no longer live in a world where it would be unthinkable for an authority figure to give a child a book in which depictions of sex, violence, drug use, profanity and the like are major elements, it is no longer safe to delegate the choice of reading material for our children to such entities as the school teacher or school librarian. Because we no longer live in a time where giving a child a book like that would be considered either child sexual abuse or contributing to the delinquency of a minor, but instead is supported with smiling approval by the moral midgets at the ALA, parents have to be more vigilant than ever. Because we no longer live in an era where we can trust the authority figures in our children's lives to share our values and foster the same view of morality and decency which we ourselves have, we can't afford to let our children read whatever trashy novel they pick up at school.

It isn't censorship to teach our children that they can't trust their teachers or librarians to give them good, wholesome books. It's just the fallout from our fractured culture, which insists on calling evil, good—and then handing it to children.

EVALUATING THE AUTHOR'S ARGUMENTS:

An important strategy in writing effective arguments is to incorporate specific examples and details to demonstrate the author's knowledge of her subject. Examine the specific details in Erin Manning's viewpoint, including statistics, book titles, and book descriptions, and explain how each one contributes to your perception of Manning's expertise.

Parents Should Restrict Only What Their Own Children Read

"I wouldn't want some other parent telling me what my daughter can read."

Dan Gutman

In the following viewpoint, children's book author Dan Gutman recounts an exchange he had with the father of one of his young readers. Although the father was angry about the language and the attitudes in one of Gutman's books, the author argues that a writer's job is to get kids excited about reading, not to teach them moral lessons. Children need to be exposed to different ideas, he concludes, and librarians need to be sure that books containing different ideas are available.

Gutman is the award-winning author of the My Weird School series and many other books for young readers.

AS YOU READ, CONSIDER THE FOLLOWING QUESTIONS:
1. What word in the first line of *Mr. Granite Is from Another Planet* does an angry parent object to, as reported by Gutman?

Dan Gutman, "How I Corrupted America's Youth: Getting Angry Letters Is No Laughing Matter—and the Same Goes for Censorship," *School Library Journal*, May 1, 2010. Copyright © 2010 by *School Library Journal.* All rights reserved. Reproduced by permission.

2. Rather than promoting hatred, what does writing about angry characters do, according to the author?
3. According to Gutman, why was Jane Yolen's book *Briar Rose* burned in Kansas City?

Recently, I received a message from a father in South Carolina—
"Hello Dan:
I double dog dare you to read this entire email and not dismiss it as some fringe, conservative wacko diatribe.

My son is seven years old and brought your book (*Mr. Granite Is from Another Planet*) up to me and said, 'Dad, this book has bad words in it.'

When I read it I was shocked at the level of depravity that spewed out of almost every thought of the characters in this book. You have propagated a literary abomination.

Do you believe that all kids think at this depraved level? My seven-year-old was repulsed at how these characters were thinking and talking. With this kind of superficial, rude content it's no wonder that young people are loading up with guns and going into schools and shooting everyone.

The first line in your book is 'My name is A.J. and I hate school.' There is no justification for feeding impressionable minds this kind of coarse, hateful thinking. At one point a girl comes up to A.J. and introduces herself and A.J's response is to call her an annoying girl and to say that he hates her. . . .

Mr. Granite Is from Another Planet is poison for young minds, and I will do everything in my power to get these books off the shelf.

Your book changed my life because now I am going to pay to send my kid to private school to protect him from a society whose morals have been eroded to a level that this kind of acrimonious dribble would even be considered much less popular."

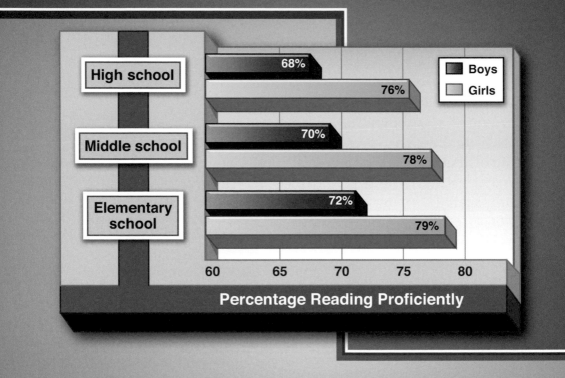

Boys Tend to Be Less Proficient at Reading Than Girls

Because fewer American boys than girls reach the "proficient" level on standardized tests of reading skills, many educators encourage schools and libraries to offer books geared toward drawing the interest of boys who are "reluctant readers."

Percentage Reading Proficiently

- High school: Boys 68%, Girls 76%
- Middle school: Boys 70%, Girls 78%
- Elementary school: Boys 72%, Girls 79%

Taken from: Center on Education Policy, "Are There Differences in Achievement Between Boys and Girls?," part 5, March 2010, p. 6.

Acrimonious Dribble

Wow! I've received some angry letters, but this one beats 'em all. Here I am, thinking "My Weird School" is a goofy series that turns on reluctant readers, when in fact I'm poisoning young minds with my depraved, acrimonious dribble.

Acrimonious Dribble?

My goal is to get kids excited about reading. In *Mr. Granite Is from Another Planet* (2008), I try to hook them with the first sentence ("My name is A.J. and I hate school."). A child who doesn't like school or reading will see that first sentence and, I hope, think "This book speaks to me. Maybe it will be different." If I've done my job, that child will open the book and become so captivated that two hours later he'll look up and not even realize he was reading.

It's human nature to find conflict more interesting than harmony. If authors just wrote perfect little angel characters who never did or said anything negative, books would be boring and kids wouldn't want to read them. To hold a child's attention and create compelling stories, we write books in which characters of opposing personalities come into conflict. Sometimes they hate each other. Just like in the real world. Having characters that get angry with one another doesn't promote hatred. It reflects reality.

[Children's author] Peg Kehret told me, "By including unethical characters, I feel I'm showing readers the bad consequences of such behavior." Peg also told me a woman tried to get her book *Abduction!* (2004) banned from every school in the district because it was too scary for her daughter.

[*Unicorn Chronicles* author] Bruce Coville, who has suffered more than his share of angry book banners, hits the nail on the head: "Somehow the idea seems to have gotten loose in the country that in addition to the rights of speech, religion, and the press we now have a new constitutional right: the right to never be offended by anything."

How Should Authors Respond?

OK, now that I've convinced myself that I'm not completely depraved, what next? Should authors respond when people send us angry letters? Not everyone agrees. Peg Kehret told me she would not have responded at all, and Lois Lowry [author of *The Giver* (1993)] says she responds to such letters politely, but "lengthy discourse on my part will not change their feelings."

Personally, I can't help myself. When someone attacks me, I have to defend myself.

I wrote back to the guy and said the beauty of America is the freedom to make our own decisions. We don't have just one person or one committee telling us how to think, what to believe, or what our kids should be allowed to read.

Freedom of speech, I insisted, means freedom from censorship. It's fine for a parent to decide his child shouldn't read a particular book. But if that parent gets the book banned from a school, they are deciding what other parents' children may or may not read. That doesn't sound fair to me. It doesn't sound American either. I wouldn't want some other parent telling me what my daughter can read.

As Bruce Coville puts it, "Withholding information is the essence of tyranny. Control of the flow of information is the tool of the dictatorship."

My first reaction, I must confess, was to laugh. I mean, get a sense-of-humor transplant, buddy! These are humor books. Of all the problems facing the world today, this guy's biggest concern is "My Weird School"? . . .

It's true that my main character, A.J., says he hates school and hates a girl in his class named Andrea. He's a mischievous little smart aleck, and that's the way kids like that talk. But readers of *My Weird School* know that A.J. is constantly being teased by his friends because he's secretly in love with Andrea. Little boys often show they like something by saying that they hate it.

After thinking it over, I decided not to worry about kids reading the word "hate" in one of my books and going off to fill the world with hatred.

I find it interesting that characters in my books have been physically attacked, kidnapped, locked in a closet, had baseball bats thrown at them, and have even been shot at, but not one parent has ever complained about violence. It's always about words. "Hate" and "butt" seem to be particularly offensive.

Jane Yolen, whose novel *Briar Rose* (1992) was burned on the steps of the Kansas City Board of Education because it features a gay character, told me, "If that parent thinks saying 'I hate school' is depraved, he is living on another planet."

The Author's Responsibility

Nearly all the complaints I receive inform me that it's my responsibility as an author to promote positive messages and moral lessons in my books. Honestly, that never even crossed my mind. I always thought it was the parent's responsibility to raise their children.

Author Dan Gutman (pictured) argues that a writer's job is to get young people excited about reading and to expose them to many points of view.

My books are purely for entertainment. I don't put "lessons" in them, at least not intentionally. Frankly, I'm suspicious of authors or authority figures that want to teach my kids morality. Morality according to whom?

In America, I continued, we get exposed to many different viewpoints. We may not like them all, but that's the price we pay to live in a democracy. The American way is to make up our own mind about what books our children should be able to read, and allow other parents to make up their own minds as well.

Told him a thing or two, huh? It seemed like an airtight argument, one that would appeal to this gentleman's patriotism. I didn't expect to hear back from him.

But I did, two days later.

The Librarian's Responsibility

"You can't yell 'fire' in a crowded theater and you can't sell kiddy porn," he informed me. "That behavior is illegal. In some cases censorship is good."

And here, I must admit, he's right. There are certain words and subjects that do not belong in a children's book. If a book is published with that material in it, somebody's got to decide how to handle it.

And that somebody, I realize, is [librarians]. . . .

Most reasonable librarians, I trust, will come down on the side of free speech over censorship and book banning. Most *SLJ* [*School Library Journal*] readers would not let a few angry, outspoken parents decide what all students should be allowed to read. I think I can speak for all authors when I say a big thank-you for the time and effort [librarians] put into carefully evaluating each challenged book and dealing with these unpleasant situations.

EVALUATING THE AUTHOR'S ARGUMENTS:

Writers of arguments often incorporate the opinions of experts to support their own claims—to show that they are not alone in what they believe. Investigate a few of the other children's authors that Dan Gutman quotes in the viewpoint you just read and their experiences with their books being banned and challenged. Which of these authors makes the greatest contribution to Gutman's case, in your opinion? Why?

Chapter 2

Should Certain Kinds of Reading Material Be Restricted?

Children's books such as You're Different and That's Super *have come under fire from antigay groups who say the books promote homosexual activism.*

Books Condoning Homosexuality Should Not Be Offered to Children

"Pro-homosexual elitists . . . are turning public, even some private, schools into pro-'gay' indoctrination zones."

Peter LaBarbera

In the following viewpoint, Peter LaBarbera describes a 2005 incident in which a Boston-area parent, David Parker, objected to a picture book that his five-year-old son brought home from school. LaBarbera argues that Parker was simply fulfilling his responsibility as a parent when he tried to prevent the school from exposing children to books about gay couples. Even though parents like Parker are mocked by the media and by liberal school officials, LaBarbera concludes, they must continue to stand up to the pro-homosexual agenda that has become a part of public education.

LaBarbera is president of Americans for Truth About Homosexuality, a group dedicated to exposing what it sees as a homosexual activist agenda.

AS YOU READ, CONSIDER THE FOLLOWING QUESTIONS:
1. What was the troublesome book that Jacob Parker brought home from school, as reported by LaBarbera?
2. What effect did Massachusetts's approving of same-sex marriage in 2004 have on the subjects discussed in school, according to the author?
3. What two alternatives to public school did Judge Mark Wolf suggest for the Parker and Wirthlin families, as cited by LaBarbera?

There is a battle to preserve right and wrong in this country— and a campaign to teach children that "human wrongs" are actually "human rights." David Parker . . . is on the front lines of that battle. . . .

Let's face it: most people sit on the sidelines in this ongoing societal "war" over *which values* will be ascendant in our culture. David and Tonia Parker got off the sidelines. When faced with a school bureaucracy in Lexington, Mass., that asserted it had the right *and duty* in the nation's only [first] homosexual-"marriage" state to teach the acceptance of homosexuality to young elementary school children without even informing parents, they fought back. In 2005, the Parkers' five-year-old son Jacob came home with a "Diversity Book Bag," which contained the book *Who's in a Family* promoting the acceptance of "same-sex" families.

The rest is history, as David Parker was famously arrested at Jacob's school, Esterbrook Elementary, for demanding his parental right to be informed before teachings that violate his and Tonia's religious beliefs were foisted on their impressionable son.

The controversy grew in 2006 when the Joseph and Robin Wirthlin learned that their seven-year-old son Joey's first-grade teacher at Esterbrook Elementary had read *King & King,* a *homosexual romance kids book* (who would think we'd ever be using those words together?) aloud to her young students without even notifying their parents.

Now the Parkers and Wirthlins are plaintiffs in a federal lawsuit against the Lexington, Massachusetts, Public Schools. The case is covered well by our good friends at MassResistance, who have created an online David Parker Report.

Prohibiting the Promotion of Homosexuality in Public Schools

According to the Sexuality Information and Education Council of the United States, seven states have policies stating that "the topic of homosexuality must not be promoted or addressed as a socially acceptable alternative to the heterosexual lifestyle" in public education.

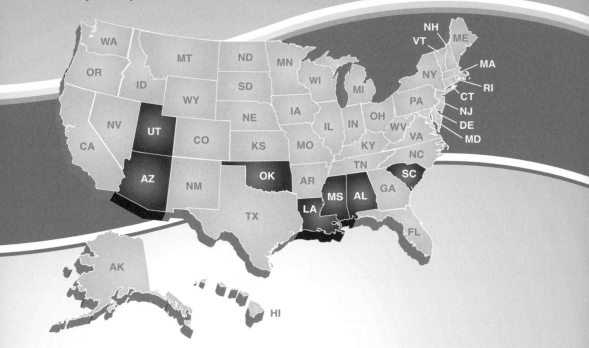

Taken from: Sexuality Information and Education Council of the United States (SIECUS), *A Portrait of Sexuality Education and Abstinence-Only-Until-Marriage Programs in the States* (Fiscal Year 2009 Edition).

Legal "Gay Marriage" Mandates Radical Lessons

Did you know that the legalization of "same-sex marriage," coupled with "sexual orientation" nondiscrimination laws, has been used by Massachusetts educators to boldly step up their teaching of homosexuality and transgenderism—using books like *King & King* that are *designed specifically to normalize homosexual behavior to young minds?* When forces in a society succeed at transforming a perversion into a "civil right," there are far-reaching ramifications—but the effect on innocent children is the most serious.

Note this summary of this National Public Radio [NPR] story about the Parker and Wirthlin case.

> Massachusetts parents infuriated that their second graders were [reading] *King & King*, a fairy tale about two gay princes, are suing the school and the teacher in federal court. The parents say schools are violating their religious freedom. But in Massachusetts, where gay marriage is legal, public school officials say they not only can talk about gay couples, they are required to.

> NPR reports that [Lexington] Superintendent [Paul] Ash said he would have "thought twice" about allowing the reading of a book like *King & King* prior to "same-sex marriage" being legalized in Massachusetts, but now he "feels both a legal and a moral obligation to teach kids about same-sex couples, and to make sure that kids of gay families don't feel like they're being treated differently." Ash continues: "I believe my job is to honor the laws of the Commonwealth of Massachusetts, and I don't think we should allow people to say, 'Well, I believe in equal rights but we don't think that *that* [lessons like reading *King & King* to second-graders] ought to be taught to children.'"

It Is Not Equal

So there it is: Gay Law 101: homosexuality-affirming legislation forces society to treat unequal things as equal—thereby corrupting and confusing even the minds of the very young. It says a lot about pro-homosexual liberals' caving moral foundation that they are increasingly willing to break down healthy and natural boundaries—even for grade school kids who don't know what *normal* sex is yet.

Celebrate the passing of older, "anti-gay" generations as you desensitize the newer ones, distorting and exploiting noble concepts like "equal rights." Since when did it become OK to expose very young children to homosexuality at all—much less through biased "lessons" that parrot the "gay" activist line?

The reasons we in the pro-family and pro-faith movement fight the homosexual activist agenda are all contained in David Parker's federal lawsuit to retain his (and all parents') right to guide their children's moral upbringing—against pro-homosexual elitists who are turning public, and even some private, schools into pro-"gay" indoctrination zones.

Radical Egalitarianism

Remember those dismissive questions posed by "gay" polemicists during homosexual "marriage" debates: "What does MY same-sex marriage have to do with your marriage?" Well, it turns out that when you revolutionize marriage through the law, you revolutionize every public institution, including schools, touching almost everyone in some way.

Radical egalitarianism—the hallmark of the Left—takes hold of sex and marriage, and soon we have the heavy hand of government enforcing a counterfeit "equality" that defies nature, reason, and common sense. Heterosexual marriage unites the sexes and naturally produces children—new life. Homosexual "unions" and their related sodomies are a dead end. (Yes, they can borrow from heterosexuality to mimic the family.) When the Left's utopian vision runs smack into the real world, children become guinea pigs and caring parents like the Parkers and the Wirthlins are thrust into the role of activists defending children's innocence and the natural order of things.

Judge Wolf's Ruling

Now read this from U.S. District Court Judge Mark Wolf's February 23 [2007] ruling dismissing the Parkers' and Wirthlins' lawsuit against Lexington Public Schools (emphasis added):

It is reasonable for public educators to teach elementary school students about individuals with different sexual orientations and about various forms of families, including those with same-sex parents, in an effort to eradicate the effects of past discrimination, to reduce the risk of future discrimination and, in the process, to reaffirm our nation's constitutional commitment to promoting mutual respect among members of our diverse society. In addition, it is reasonable for those educators to find that *teaching young children to understand and respect differences in sexual orientation* will contribute to an academic environment in which students who are gay, lesbian, or the children of same-sex parents will be comfortable and, therefore, better able to learn.

The Parkers and Wirthlins may send their children to a private school that does not seek to foster understandings of homosexuality or same-sex marriage that conflict with their religious beliefs. They may also educate their children at home.

Translation: if you don't like our version of "tolerance," then leave. . . .

Get Parents Out of the Way

Somewhere along the line, teachers evolved into "change agents" (another leftist term) and Judeo-Christian morality became the target of social revolutionaries.

When their five-year-old son brought a book about gay couples home from school, David and Tonia Parker (pictured) sued school officials in Lexington, Massachusetts. Their case was ultimately dismissed by a US district court judge.

But just having edgy lessons is not enough: to change developing, malleable minds, you need to preempt and circumvent those pesky parents. In the words of the author of *Who's in a Family*:

The whole purpose of the book was to get the subject [of same-sex parent households] out into the minds and the awareness of children before they are old enough to have been convinced that there's another way of looking at life. . . . It would be really nice if children were not subjected to the—I don't want to use the word 'bigotry,' but that's what I want to say anyway—of their parents and older people.

David and Tonia Parker are fighting just for the basic right to be informed about what is being taught to their child. If Judge Wolf's troubling ruling is not overturned, another legal precedent will be established that says public school parents need not even be informed about—much less be able to guide—the curriculum of their child's classroom teachings that may clash with their moral beliefs. [In October 2008, the US Supreme Court declined to hear an appeal of Judge Wolf's ruling, ending the case.]

EVALUATING THE AUTHOR'S ARGUMENTS:

Writers of arguments sometimes use a device known as "scare quotes," or quotation marks around certain words or phrases; typically, writers use these marks to show that they do not agree with how others use the words. For example, in the viewpoint you have just read, Peter LaBarbera uses quotation marks around the words "gay" and "marriage," to show that he does not like the term "gay" as applied to homosexual people and that he does not consider their unions to be equal to marriage. How does this technique affect your reading of the argument and your reaction to the author?

Sexual Orientation Is an Important Part of the Elementary School Curriculum

"Anti-bias programs do not try to change . . . deeply held views, but ensure that the diversity of opinions in school communities [does] not create a negative climate."

GroundSpark

The following viewpoint argues that it is important to address lesbian, gay, bisexual, and transgender (LGBT) issues with children. Many students have LGBT parents or other relatives, the author explains, and even children in elementary school face teasing and bullying from peers who have not yet learned to respect all families. Age-appropriate discussions about respect and cooperation and other core values should be acceptable to all cultures, GroundSpark concludes, and parents should not be allowed to exclude their children from these lessons.

GroundSpark is an organization that produces films and educational resources on issues ranging from environmental concerns to affordable housing to preventing prejudice. In 1996 the group released the film *It's Elementary: Talking About Gay Issues in School.*

AS YOU READ, CONSIDER THE FOLLOWING QUESTIONS:
1. What happens when teachers do not comment about antigay slurs, according to the authors?
2. During the 1990s, where did schools generally conduct discussions about lesbian, gay, bisexual, and transgendered people, as reported by GroundSpark?
3. According to the authors, what has happened to some schools that did not provide a safe environment for all their students?

W*hy is LGBT-inclusive curriculum necessary?*
Sadly, homophobia and heterosexism are still very much present in many of our schools and communities. These biases manifest themselves [in] many ways, from invisibility in the curriculum and school policies to active teasing, bullying, harassment and physical violence against gender variant children, youth who identify as lesbian, gay, bisexual or transgender (LGBT), and families that include LGBT parents or relatives. This bias hurts all children, both those directly affected and those who learn in an atmosphere of fear and tension, afraid to explore their own lives because of worry about disapproval and rejection. Students of all ages must be given an opportunity to learn that the words "gay" and "lesbian" are adjectives that should be used with respect to describe people in their community, not words used in a negative way to hurt, insult and degrade. Students need to be encouraged to reflect on their own actions and prejudice, learn from their peers who are different from them and support allies who stand up to prejudice and hate. Creating inclusive curriculum and establishing accepting classroom and school climates improves the educational experience for all students, families and teachers.

Are Elementary Kids Too Young for This?

Are elementary school children too young to be introduced to this topic?

Unfortunately name-calling and using anti-gay slurs starts as early as kindergarten, first and second grades. . . . Children at a very young age have already been introduced to information about LGBT people, which is often based on misinformation and negative stereotypes. When teachers are silent about gay and lesbian people, students learn from this omission that it is acceptable to use anti-gay put-downs. Anti-gay slurs are hurtful and unacceptable and they affect the lives of people in every school and community. Teachers are not introducing a new topic, they are helping young students understand bias and prejudice and learn to use respectful language. Educators are creating inclusive school communities that prevent name-calling, teasing and bullying and provide safe learning environments for all children.

Do parents and guardians need to be notified if LGBT people or families are discussed in the classroom?

In many school districts, there are guidelines about what classroom activities require parent/guardian notification. Most school districts do not have a requirement for notifying parents and guardians for lessons about respect and diversity. In fact, many districts require schools to be proactive in addressing bias and prejudice and ensuring students' safety. Discussions related to sexuality and reproduction are examples of topics that often require parental permission. . . . The focus of

Due to a climate of homophobia and heterosexism in many schools, supporters of lesbian, gay, bisexual, and transgender (LGBT) kids say that including LGBT curriculum is needed to provide these students with a safe learning environment.

LGBT-inclusive education is to create respectful and welcoming learning environments for all children by communicating that LGBT people are part of our communities and that anti-LGBT discrimination is harmful to everyone. However, we strongly recommend involving parents and guardians as part of school-wide efforts to be more inclusive. As important members of the school community, families can help reinforce the concepts of respect at home, help answer questions,

Lesbian, Gay, Bisexual, and Transgender Students Face Harassment at School

In a 2009 survey of middle school and high school lesbian, gay, bisexual, and transgendered (LGBT) students, many reported that they had been verbally harassed, physically harassed (pushed or shoved), or physically assaulted (punched, kicked, or injured with a weapon) at school because of their sexual orientation.

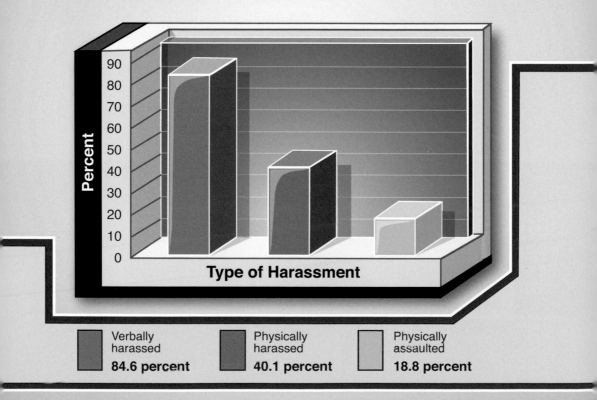

Verbally harassed
84.6 percent

Physically harassed
40.1 percent

Physically assaulted
18.8 percent

Taken from: Gay, Lesbian and Straight Education Network (GLSEN), *The 2009 National School Climate Survey*, Executive Summary, 2010, p.3.

assist in classroom discussions and be actively engaged in making the school and community safe for all children and their families.

Can Parents Opt Out?

Can parents/guardians "opt out" of their children's participation in school instruction that includes LGBT-inclusive lessons?

Most school districts have limited and clear guidelines about offering parents and guardians the right to have their children "opt out" of specific school instruction. Programs that are designed to encourage respect and address bias typically are not included in "opt out" policies. By not including all students in LGBT-inclusive lessons, schools run the risk of conveying a message that it is somehow acceptable to engage in hurtful and disrespectful behavior when it comes to LGBT people. We strongly discourage schools from allowing students to miss lessons where people and families—not sexual practices—are discussed. Oftentimes those students are among those who might benefit the most from being with their peers when community values around respect and understanding are addressed.

> **FAST FACT**
>
> In a survey conducted by the Gay, Lesbian and Straight Education Network in 2008–2009, 22 percent of students with gay, lesbian, bisexual, or transgendered parents said that a teacher, principal, or other school staff person had discouraged them from talking about their family at school.

How do we comply with antidiscrimination laws and still respect the religious and cultural diversity of our students and their families?

Simply stated, an anti-bias program is designed to create a space in which all students can learn, achieve their goals, and realize success. Anti-bias curriculum encourages respect, cooperation and understanding, values that all religions and cultures hold in common. In fact, by giving students a language to discuss these sensitive issues, families may find it easier to share their own religious beliefs about human difference. Anti-bias programs do not try to change those deeply held views, but ensure that the diversity of opinions in school communities do not create a negative climate of insults, violence, and exclusion. Part of that work is ensuring that children can be proud of their own religious and cultural heritage without being marginalized.

Not the Same as Sex Education

Is talking about LGBT issues the same as sex education?

Talking about LGBT issues is a discussion about people and families present in our communities, a struggle for civil rights and addressing bias-based bullying. None of these include talking about sex or human reproduction. Many educators once feared that the two were inseparable, and schools in the 1990s typically limited discussions about LGBT people to high school health classes. However, with the rapid growth of LGBT-headed families and the increasing visibility of LGBT issues in the media, children are learning about LGBT people at an increasingly younger age. . . .

What if our anti-bias education programs that are LGBT-inclusive cause controversy in the community?

Misunderstandings about the purpose and content of anti-bias education programs can happen in any community. It is important to be transparent and open about the intentions and content of the program to avoid accusations that it is part of a larger, hidden "agenda." In fact, you can actually strengthen the bonds of your school community by involving families in your family diversity and anti-bias programs. It is also important to have the support of your school and community leaders, not just to prevent controversy, but also to strengthen the actual work of your program. Key school staff such as principals, counselors and department chairs should be familiar with the content of your program before it is implemented, and understand the reasons why you are doing so. PTA [Parent Teacher Association] chapters are also an often-overlooked source of support, as are church and youth organizations, and local colleges of education. Members of these groups can provide professional input as to why your program is needed, while also offering insights on how it can be delivered. If a controversy does arise, it is important to communicate to families that your anti-bias program is supported, or even mandated, by state law and educational policies. Many states and school districts have an anti-harassment policy that includes sexual orientation, or require their staff to receive anti-bias training. Academic standards also often require teaching about diversity in communities and families. Schools have an obligation to ensure all their students are able to learn in a safe environment, and recent court decisions have delivered costly verdicts to schools that fail to do so. Overall, it is important to stand firm on your commitment to addressing biases of all kinds. School districts that have bowed to pressure in the past have only seen the controversy intensify, as new attacks are levied against other curricula and school programs connected to sensitive subjects.

EVALUATING THE AUTHOR'S ARGUMENTS:

The two viewpoints you have just read address many of the same issues, but it appears that their authors would be unable to communicate effectively with each other. Do you think the authors from GroundSpark would recognize their anti-bias curriculum in the descriptions offered by Peter LaBarbera? Would LaBarbera be reassured by GroundSpark's claim that their curriculum would make it easier for families like the Parkers and Wirthlins "to share their own religious beliefs"? What strategies might writers use in their arguments to make themselves heard and respected by those who strongly disagree with them?

Parents Should Challenge Books Containing Inappropriate Language

"It is even more important today in a culture in which profanity, obscenity, and sexual imagery relentlessly bombard our youth that schools stand as one of the last bastions of integrity, civility, and temperance."

Laurie Higgins

In the following viewpoint, Laurie Higgins, a high school teacher, walks the reader through common objections parents often hear from educators when they challenge books that their children read in school, and she provides answers that parents might give in response to these objections. Although teachers and librarians might claim that profane and obscene words should be accepted in books because they are part of the language students encounter in the world, Higgins argues that the language—especially when it is encountered in the supposedly safe environment of school—is harmful to young readers. If educators will not offer appropriate books, she concludes, then parents must step in and insist that they do.

Laurie Higgins, "Answers to Liberal Teachers' Arguments—for Parents Challenging Objectionable Books in Schools," AmericansforTruth.com, August 24, 2007. Copyright © 2007 by Americans for Truth About Homosexuality. All rights reserved. Reproduced by permission.

When she wrote this viewpoint, Higgins worked in the writing center at Deerfield High School, a public school outside Chicago. She now works with the Illinois Family Institute, a group that works to promote and defend biblical ideals.

AS YOU READ, CONSIDER THE FOLLOWING QUESTIONS:
1. According to Higgins, why are many parents and teachers unlikely to admit that obscene and profane language is inappropriate?
2. What is meant by the term "moral development," as used by the author?
3. As reported by Higgins, how many books will a typical student read in four years of high school English classes?

As a new school year begins, here are some of the arguments that parents may encounter when they challenge books (e.g. *The Chocolate War, Fat Kid Rules the World, The Laramie Project,* or *Angels in America: A Gay Fantasia on National Themes*) for their problematic ideological messages, the nature and extent of profanity and obscenity, or the nature and extent of depictions of sexuality, followed by brief responses.

Parents who challenge a book because of language need to bear in mind that many of the parents and teachers who approve of these objectionable texts use the same obscene and profane language commonly and casually in their personal lives, even with their children, though they will not likely admit it. Therefore, it is highly unlikely that they will concede that profanity and obscenity are objectionable, for conceding that would constitute a personal indictment:

Parents are taking words out of context, and it is the context that justifies the language.

Response: There is no context that renders frequent and excessively obscene language acceptable in texts selected by public school teachers for minor children. In other words, the extreme nature and pervasiveness of obscenity renders the entire text unsuitable for public schools whose mission is to cultivate the best behavior in students.

Profane and obscene language is justified because it represents authentic adolescent language.

Response: If the author is justified in using this language to portray authentically adolescent culture and the emotional experiences of adolescents, then surely students are justified in using this language in school in order to be authentic and to express adequately and accurately their emotional truths. Teachers too should be allowed to use this language because it also represents authentic adult language and experience. In fact, society often erroneously and euphemistically refers to profanity and obscenity as "adult language."

The Prevalence of Foul Language

Counting numbers of swear words constitutes an immature or silly evaluative mechanism.

Response: Taking into account the extent of foul language is neither silly nor juvenile. There is a substantive difference between one incident of "f**k" and one hundred. The incessant drumbeat of obscenities desensitizes readers to their offensiveness and normalizes their use. Moreover, although adults may distinguish between literary use and endorsement, many adolescents do not.

First, the prevalence of foul language should be taken into account. Second, the nature of the obscenity or profanity should be taken into account. Third, who is using the offensive language should be taken into account. Is it the hero or the antagonist? Fourth, parents and educators should realize that books with profuse obscenity and the willingness of educators to teach them convey the message that there are justifiable reasons and contexts for using extremely foul language.

Since students mature at different rates, some students are mature enough for these texts. Parents, therefore, should decide what is appropriate for their child.

Response: Whoever makes this argument should be asked to define maturity. If they are referring to intellectual development, then it is irrelevant to the discussion in that parents who challenge texts because of language, sexuality, or pro-homosexual messages, are not doing so because they find the material intellectually inaccessible. If educators are referring to emotional maturity, meaning that students are emotionally stable enough to read and discuss emotionally difficult material without being traumatized, that too is likely irrelevant, for few parents who object to language, sexuality, or pro-homosexual messages are concerned that their children will be emotionally traumatized.

Parents Concerned with Moral Development

The concern conservative parents have is with moral development. They recognize that all adolescents, including even mature high school seniors, are not yet adults. They are still constructing a moral compass. They are impressionable, malleable, and much more vulnerable to external influences than are adults whose moral compass is likely fixed and stable. For a teacher to contend that there is any 12–18 year-old whose moral compass is fully developed, mature, and fixed represents an ignorant and hubristic assertion.

Every parent should be able to send their child to school confident that their beliefs regarding decency and morality will not be challenged by educators or curricula, especially since this confidence can be secured without compromising the academic enterprise. It is even more important today in a culture in which profanity, obscenity, and sexual imagery relentlessly bombard our youth that schools stand as one of the last bastions of integrity, civility, and temperance. . . .

> ## FAST FACT
>
> Of the 10,676 challenges in the American Library Association's 1990–2010 Challenge Database, 6,103 were brought by parents.

This book has won prestigious literary awards or has been approved by the American Library Association (ALA).

Response: This justification begs the question: Who serves on committees that award prizes or review texts? And this argument calls for a serious, open, and honest examination of the ideological monopoly that controls academia and the elite world of the arts that for decades has engaged in censorship of conservative scholarship. To offer as justification for teaching a text the garnering of literary prizes or ALA

"Excuse me, Sir, but none of us has any money left to buy lunch."

approval without acknowledging that those who award the prizes and belong to the ALA are generally of the same ideological bent is an exercise in sophistry.

What school committees, departments, administrations, school boards, the ALA, the National Education Association (NEA), and organizations that award literary prizes desperately need is the one form of diversity about which they are least concerned and to which they are least committed: idcological diversity.

Pandering to Kids' Tastes

Kids relate to this book and, therefore, it captures and holds their interest.

Response: If this criterion has assumed a dominant place in the selection process, then teachers have abandoned their proper role as educators. Appealing to the sensibilities and appetites of adolescents should not be the goal of educators. There's another word for capitulating to the tastes of adolescents: it is called pandering. Schools should teach those texts that students will likely not read on their own. We should teach those texts that are intellectually challenging and offer insight, wisdom, beauty, and truth. We should avoid those that are highly polemical, blasphemous, and vulgar.

To remove this text constitutes censorship.

Response: Parents who object to the inclusion of texts on recommended or required reading lists due to obscene language, sexuality, or highly controversial messages are not engaging in some kind of inappropriate censorship. All educators evaluate curricular materials for objectionable content, including language, sexuality, and controversial themes. The irony is that when teachers decide not to select a text due to these elements, the choice constitutes an exercise in legitimate decision-making, but when parents engage in it, they are tarred with the label of "censor."

Furthermore, virtually no parents advocate prior restraint and only rarely are they asking for the removal of a text from a school library. Rather, parents are suggesting that it is reasonable to include the nature and extent of profanity, obscenity, and sexuality when selecting texts to be recommended and/or taught to minors in public schools.

Are those teachers, administrators, and school board members who disagree with that suggestion saying that they will never take into account the nature and extent of profanity, obscenity, and sexuality? If they are claiming that they will never take into account these elements, then parents should reconsider their fitness for teaching.

In all four years of high school English, students read approximately 28–32 books. From the dozens and dozens of texts available, it seems unlikely that any student's education would be compromised by teachers', in the service of respect for parental values, comity, and modesty, avoiding the most controversial texts.

EVALUATING THE AUTHOR'S ARGUMENTS:

The viewpoints in this book have been written by a number of people with different backgrounds: parents, librarians, authors, religious figures, and college professors. The viewpoint you have just read was written by public high school teacher Laurie Higgins. How does a writer's occupation or role in a controversy affect how you read his or her argument? In the particular case of this viewpoint, how is Higgins's role as a staff member in a public school likely to inform her argument?

Viewpoint

4

Anatomical Names for Body Parts Are Not Offensive

Susan Patron

> "Our society is filled with appalling acts, images, and events from which we would like to shield children, but this is not possible— because children live in the same world we inhabit."

In the following viewpoint, children's book author Susan Patron describes the controversy that followed the announcement that her novel *The Higher Power of Lucky* had won the prestigious Newbery Medal. Many adults objected to the word "scrotum" that appears on the first page, she explains, and some librarians then hesitated to add the book to their collections out of worry that challenges would follow. Novels for young people, Patron argues, should invite them to ask difficult—even uncomfortable—questions about themselves and their world, and adults should not limit children's access to good books because of individual words, particularly names of body parts.

Patron, the author of eight children's books, worked for thirty-five years as a librarian in Los Angeles.

Susan Patron, "Shock Treatment," *Horn Book Magazine,* vol. 85, no. 5, October 2009, pp. 481–483, 486.

In *Quirkology: How We Discover the Big Truths in Small Things,* the author, Richard Wiseman, tells the following story. A man goes to a psychiatrist. The shrink shows the man a stack of cards containing inkblots and asks him to say what the inkblots remind him of. The man looks at the first inkblot and says, "Sex." He looks at the second inkblot and says, "Sex." He goes through the whole stack, saying the word *sex* in response each time. The psychiatrist says, "I don't wish to worry you, but you seem to have sex on your mind." The man looks surprised, and answers, "I can't believe you just said that—*you're* the one with all the dirty pictures!"

This joke made me think about the reaction to a passage on page one of my novel *The Higher Power of Lucky,* in which a dog is bitten on the scrotum by a rattlesnake. A nationwide controversy erupted about it shortly after the announcement that *Lucky* had won the 2007 Newbery Award, prompted by some exchanges on the listserv LM_NET, which reaches some 16,000 school librarians. *Publishers Weekly* ran an article on these posts, including one by a Colorado teacher-librarian who wrote, "This book included what I call a Howard Stern–type shock treatment [radio host Howard Stern is known for shocking material] just to see how far they could push the envelope, but they didn't have the children in mind. How very sad." She goes on to say, "I don't want to start an issue about censorship. But you won't find men's genitalia in quality literature . . . at least not for children."

"Fear," [novelist] Judy Blume says on her website, "is often disguised as moral outrage."

Which Words Raise Objections?

I had flown from Los Angeles to New York City the day after the Newbery announcement to appear (for maybe fourteen seconds) on the *Today* [television] show. Afterward, [book publisher] Simon & Schuster took me to a swank restaurant for lunch. The director of publicity said that we'd all need to get used to the word *scrotum*. So we all chanted, "Scrotum, scrotum, scrotum," while the waiter stood by with a bored expression on his face. That was the first of many surreal experiences I would encounter during the year. And the publicist was right.

In my earlier chapter book, *Maybe Yes, Maybe No, Maybe Maybe,* written for an even younger audience, I had used the word *uterus*. The book was an ALA [American Library Association] Notable Book and made several "best of the year" lists. No one ever raised the issue of the word *uterus* or worried about its effect on eight-year-old children. What was different with *scrotum* in *Lucky?* The editor of both books, Richard Jackson, says *uterus* is a girl word, so it's less scary than a boy word. I think, also, that some adults evidently feel that the Newbery should be "safe." By *safe* I mean a book that doesn't reflect the world in which children live; a book without words that might make readers ask potentially uncomfortable questions. Of course, this is precisely what literature *should* do. It should invite children to explore their own hearts and the mysteries of the universe. Our society is filled with appalling acts, images, and events from which we would like to shield children, but this is not possible—because children live in the same world we inhabit. In my own books, I want to offer hope as well—not false hope or over-sentimentalized solutions, but the idea that we humans can make choices and we can redeem ourselves through those choices.

> **FAST FACT**
>
> Banned Books Week, held during the last week in September each year, is sponsored by the American Library Association, the American Booksellers Foundation for Free Expression, the Association of American Publishers, the American Society of Journalists and Authors, and the National Association of College Stores.

But it seemed that some professionals were determining the appropriateness of a book on the basis of its first page. Rather than looking at the work as a whole, these practitioners—many admitting they hadn't read the book—paused instead to ask, What if parents or the school board object?

What Adults and Children See

I found myself in a position so ironic it was dizzying. For over twenty-five years, in my collection development work at the Los Angeles Public Library, part of my job was to respond to challenges that had not been resolved at the local branch level; I'd trained new children's librarians on handling complaints and on the importance of controversial materials being included in all collections. We always discussed ALA's Code of Ethics, especially number VII: "We distinguish between our personal convictions and professional duties and do not allow our personal beliefs to interfere with fair representation of the aims of our institutions or the provision of access to their . . . resources." Book selection must be responsive to "the aims of our institutions" rather than a matter of our personal preferences or convictions—such as the conviction that a child should not read the name of certain body parts in a work of fiction.

I was *so* grounded in the concepts of freedom of access and intellectual freedom for kids, and *so* passionate about defending these freedoms. But suddenly it was different: This was *my own book.* I wasn't a librarian; I was a writer. I felt intensely vulnerable. I wanted to go everywhere wearing lots of armor, draping myself with those Newbery seals that both sparked the controversy and shielded the book from its effects. But here's the amazing thing: Many of the children who came to bookstores and libraries while I was on a promotional tour that year had already read the book, and although they had rich, thoughtful questions, not one of them asked about the dog's scrotum. They had read the book on a more emotional level: They wanted to know why Lucky is called Lucky; they wanted to know about Lincoln and Lucky's friendship and about Miles's mother who is in jail.

My experiences on the road were echoed in letters and e-mails; this one, for example, from a school librarian in Chicago: "Next week is Banned Books Week, and I do a huge bulletin board with activities

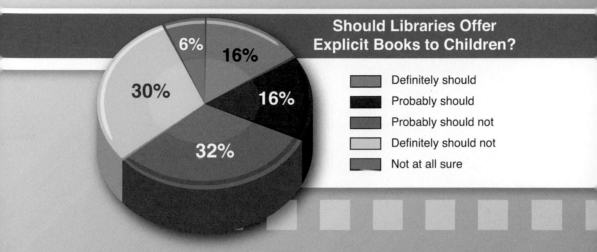

School Libraries and Explicit Language

In a 2011 survey of 2,379 adults, 62 percent said that school libraries probably or definitely should not offer books with explicit language to children.

Should Libraries Offer Explicit Books to Children?

6%
16%
30%
16%
32%

- Definitely should
- Probably should
- Probably should not
- Definitely should not
- Not at all sure

Taken from: Harris Interactive, press release, April 12, 2011.

for grades 6–8. I talk about the reasons people challenge books, and try to get the kids to see it from the 'challenging' parents' point of view. I gave each group a book to present. They needed to tell the others why their book might be controversial and then defend the book. One book was *The Higher Power of Lucky.* I told them to find the controversy; it's on the first page. They couldn't find it. They read right over it, unfazed by the word, and had to look online to find out what the fuss was about." . . .

Many people asked me whether I had the rattlesnake bite the dog on its scrotum, rather than some other place, in order to generate sales or to shock à la Howard Stern. The answer is that I have way too much respect for the intelligence and sensibilities of children ever to be that cynical. In fact, the word *scrotum* was very deliberately and carefully chosen. I needed to give Lucky a sensitive, slightly taboo question to which she wants an answer, and it was crucial to show that at the beginning of the book she feels she has no one she can ask.

When, in a pivotal scene at the end of the book, she is finally able to ask her guardian Brigitte the meaning of *scrotum,* the reader knows that we have come to a place of great trust and love. And we realize this is because Lucky has found the parent to whom she can openly pose questions and from whom she'll get candid and straightforward responses.

EVALUATING THE AUTHOR'S ARGUMENTS:

Toward the end of her viewpoint, Susan Patron explains that she included the word *scrotum* because she wanted something "sensitive, slightly taboo" for her character Lucky to struggle with. Do you agree that the names of some parts of the body are "sensitive, slightly taboo"? Where would you draw the line between language that is appropriate for students in middle school to read and to use and language that is not appropriate? Do you think you and your peers would draw the line in the same place that your parents or teachers would draw it? Explain.

Reading About Obscene or Frightening Reality Is Harmful to Young People

Alba English and Paula Silvey

"What are we giving our kids to 'dream' about by exposing them to this vulgar subject matter?"

The authors of the following viewpoint, Alba English and Paula Silvey, describe a meeting at which a group of women discussed controversial books assigned in a local high school and shared strategies for challenging the use of those books. It is the responsibility of all citizens, the authors argue, to protect children from vulgar and graphic reading material—material that is likely to lead them to destructive behaviors, including suicide. Parents must contact their local school boards, they conclude, and demand that only high-quality materials be used in schools.

English is a director with Concerned Women for America of Kansas, a coalition of conservative women that promotes biblical and traditional family values. Silvey is a prayer action leader with the same organization.

AS YOU READ, CONSIDER THE FOLLOWING QUESTIONS:
1. What background did Janet Harmon bring to her analysis of reading materials, as described by the authors?
2. As suggested by English and Silvey, what has happened to the teen suicide rate?
3. Why, according to the school board member who attended the meeting described by the authors, did the school board fail to supervise the reading selections of English classes?

On Thursday, September 9, 2004, we attended the monthly meeting of the Sunflower Republican Women's Club in Overland Park, Kansas. This was not your ordinary meeting. This was a standing-room-only crowd. Nancy Hanahan, the club's President, had invited a parent in the Blue Valley School system, Janet Harmon, as well as School Board member Cheryl Spalding to be the guest speakers. The topic was the "required reading" books that this school system has approved for its English classes.

Janet, who heads a group called "Citizens for Literary Standards in Schools," spoke first and discussed whether it really matters what children read and whether this kind of reading is age-appropriate. She came at this from the perspective of a parent as well as a former English teacher herself. She was sincere in her concerns and articulated her reasons for challenging some of the books being used. But the most powerful part of her presentation was the handout that she provided containing excerpts from the books in question.

> ## FAST FACT
> The Centers for Disease Control and Prevention reports that suicide is the third leading cause of death for people aged fifteen to twenty-four.

Now I realize that some of you reading this article are going to scream the usual rhetoric . . . "you right-wing radicals, you just want to censor everything our kids need to read." I say to your smoke screen, get off of it. We are parents, we are grandparents, we are stakeholders in this school system, we are educators, we are voters and taxpayers and our concern for our kids goes far deeper than the politics of this issue. We ask, "are we really protecting our children?"

Dangerous Exposure

Recently a national study was funded by the Rand Corporation, which showed that kids who are exposed to explicit sex on television are more likely to experiment with what they see. We contend that the same conclusion can be drawn here with regard to the school's required reading list. The kids *are* "affected" by what they read. We can all remember as kids reading wonderful fiction and non-fiction and being transported in our minds to those far-away places, doing what the characters did and experiencing vicariously what the characters

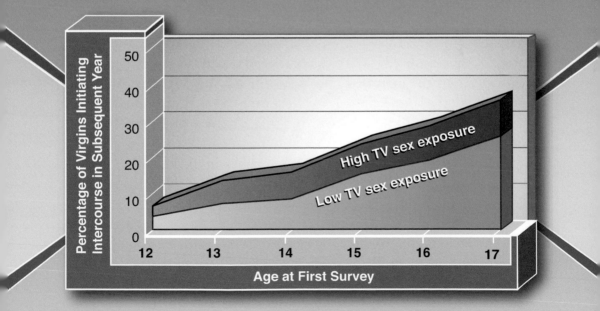

Sex: Television Exposure and Experimentation

According to a study conducted by the Rand Corporation, teens who saw a lot of sex on television were more likely to begin having sex themselves than teens who saw little or no sex on television.

Percentage of Virgins Initiating Intercourse in Subsequent Year

High TV sex exposure

Low TV sex exposure

Age at First Survey

Taken from: Rand Corporation, "Does Watching Sex on Television Influence Teens' Sexual Activity?," 2004.

The author is a director of Concerned Women For America. Here, a member presents the group's opposition to legislation expanding North Dakota's hate crimes law.

experienced. Has something changed? What are we giving our kids to "dream" about by exposing them to this vulgar subject matter, prolific use of obscenities, sexually stimulating passages, graphic descriptions of rape, incest, pedophilia, oral sex, anal sex, bestiality and violence? We wonder about the increased rate of suicide among our teens, but we fail to make the connection. We expect them to read these books and yet to separate it from their own thinking. Are we not "contributing to the delinquency of a minor"?

You can parade all the teens you want before us and have them testify of how wonderful these books are and how they should not be censored, and how great the teacher presented the materials and how necessary this or that book was in order to teach a particular concept like "persuasion" or "critical thinking," but we don't buy it for a minute. Many students and teachers have been so "de-sensitized" that they think of the reading of these books as a "right."

Wake Up, Parents!

It's time for parents to wake up and look in the mirror. What's coming up is much closer than you think—increased suicide among teens, increased STDs [sexually transmitted diseases], reckless and thoughtless behavior. Must there continue to be a downward spiral? The use of these books has been promoted by THOSE who think they know better than YOU do what is best for YOUR child. At this meeting the school board member confessed that these books came into the system because the focus of the Board over the last few years has been on facilities planning and budgets, not on curriculum. To that the Sunflower Club president stated that "somebody's been in the back seat and there's been no driver."

Wake up, parents! There are many excellent books (some of them on the curriculum list, some of them classics) that could be used to teach critical thinking skills. If we really want to do what is good for the children, we will require a higher standard of literature in our schools. We will be concerned both for their "physical safety" as well as their "mental safety." We will not continue to permit this "assault" and "abuse" on our children's minds with amoral and immoral literature.

EVALUATING THE AUTHOR'S ARGUMENTS:

The viewpoint you have just read is unusual in its approach. Alba English and Paula Silvey use the word *we* almost twenty times to describe concerned parents and citizens, and frequently use the word *you* to directly confront those who disagree with the viewpoint's arguments. The last paragraph begins with the emotional "Wake up, parents!" It emphasizes words by putting them in all capital letters or between quotation marks. How do these dramatic and emotional techniques affect your perception of the writers and your reading of their viewpoint?

Authors of Young Adult Books Have Good Reasons for Depicting Gritty but Realistic Events

"Authors feel strongly compelled to be honest with their readers, much like one might imagine a frank discussion between a parent and a child."

Rebecca Hill

In the viewpoint that follows, Rebecca Hill explains why authors of novels for young adults so often address controversial issues, including abuse, prostitution, and drug use. These authors have learned, she argues, that teens have a strong need for books that depict the realities of the harsh world in which many of them live, especially if the books can provide a measure of hopefulness. Feedback from teen readers proves, she concludes, that anything less than honesty would disappoint them and would teach them the wrong lessons.

Hill is a librarian and writer who focuses on libraries, literacy, and other educational issues.

Most authors write without the constant worry that someone will object to what they have written. No one is looking over their shoulders, questioning the appropriateness of their prose or the topics on which they choose to write. But in current young adult [YA] literature circles, a small group of authors are writing with that shadow of censorship over their heads. Hundreds of challenges arise every year, and the impact can be devastating, not only to the teachers and librarians who must face them but also to the writers of the challenged books. Author Judy Blume is very experienced with these issues. In her book *Places I Never Meant to Be: Original Stories by Censored Writers*, Blume muses about the time she wrote *Are You There God? It's Me, Margaret*: "Controversy wasn't on my mind. I wanted only to write what I knew to be true. I wanted to write the best, the most honest books I could, the kinds of books I would have liked to read when I was younger. If someone had told me then [that] I would become one of the most banned writers in America, I'd have laughed." But if hindsight is indeed [twenty-twenty], the question remains why any author who writes about controversial subjects for teens would even venture to do so? . . .

FAST FACT

The South Carolina Department of Mental Health reports that 95 percent of those who have eating disorders in the United States are between twelve and twenty-five years old.

The Gamut of Controversial Subjects

These so-called radical reads cover the gamut of controversial subject matter. From sex to rape, teen pregnancy, homosexuality, drugs, suicide,

Author Judy Blume has won numerous awards for her young adult books, but conservative activists have been successful in getting many of them banned.

violence, and even murder, this onslaught of realism would be a slap in the face if these problems weren't very real issues that teens cope with in today's society. Looking at the daily headlines, the reality explodes off the page. Teen suicide is the third leading cause of death among young adults, and homicide is the second leading cause of death. Juveniles account for almost 16 percent of all violent crime arrests. Approximately 75 percent of students will have consumed alcohol by the end of high school. Nearly 50 percent of teens will have tried cigarettes by twelfth grade, and 25 percent of seniors will have used illicit drugs. And although we might long for a *Betsy and Tacy* or *Hardy Boys* existence for our teens, the honest fact is that they face very real issues and reading about those issues in fiction can help create coping mechanisms.

Depicting Stark Realities

It is from these very real issues that the stories evolve. Whether it is from a stark statistic on teenage prostitution or a letter from an anorexic teenage girl now in treatment—what these authors imagine to be the story behind these realities is what motivates them. When Patricia McCormick first wrote her book *Cut,* no one was writing about the issue of teens who were cutting. She felt driven to write a novel on this topic and frame it from a girl's point of view.

"I felt like it was something both fascinating and really upsetting and needed to be told from the girl's point of view," McCormick said. "My feeling was that there was so much judgment and so much repulsion about the topic. Most people didn't know anything about it."

For her most recent book, *Wintergirls,* [Laurie Halse] Anderson found her inspiration in the stories of her readers. She heard from teens who were experiencing eating disorders or who were receiving treatment for them. "So many of my readers wrote to me about their struggles with eating disorders," Anderson says, "and after speaking with a very close doctor friend of mine, I began to tell Lia's story."

For Ellen Hopkins, author of *Crank, Glass, Impulse,* and *Burned,* it was a mere statistic that shocked her into the story of teenage prostitution. These types of subjects, she believes, touch the lives of teens more than we generally know.

"With *Tricks,* I read a statistic that the average age of a teen prostitute in the United States is twelve years old," Hopkins says. "When I come across something like this, I have to go figure out why. Then I start researching. Mostly, I think that it is important that we look at these issues. It is easy enough to pretend that they don't happen—to try [to] hide them in the closet or corner somewhere, but they do. The only way to skew those statistics back up where we want them is by investigating and asking why."

Compelled to Be Honest

These authors feel strongly compelled to be honest with their readers, much like one might imagine a frank discussion between a parent and a child. For teens, hearing these stories and reading about the possible realities of poor choices can demonstrate that the monsters they encounter, whether supernatural or human, "can be killed, vanquished, learned from, and overcome," says [author Joni Richards] Bodart. "That's why YA authors write radical reads, and that's why teens read them. [Teens] need to know that the monsters can be killed and that they can survive even the worst of them, if they choose to do so. They also need to know that they aren't alone—there's at least one person out there [who] . . . understands them and what they are living with."

And because they deal with subject matter that is painfully intimate, reader feedback can illustrate the overwhelming responsibility that these authors have. Hopkins says that failing to be honest about what happens to her characters when they make questionable decisions will only lead her readers to point out this fact. "If I don't write honestly about [the issue] then I'm just another person saying 'don't do it.' I have to show that it's fun until it's not fun anymore. Because [it's] the truth. I hopefully write the truth. My readers will call me on it if I don't."

EVALUATING THE AUTHOR'S ARGUMENTS:

In the viewpoint you have just read by Rebecca Hill and the previous viewpoint by Alba English and Paula Silvey, the authors look at some of the same pieces of evidence but draw completely opposite conclusions from them. English and Silvey list several controversial behaviors and conclude that exposure to these behaviors in books and on television causes teens to experiment with them, leading to harm. Hill also includes a list of controversial subject matter but concludes that reading about these behaviors—which, she says, are already part of many teens' lives—helps teens cope with troubling issues. Can both viewpoints be right? How should a reader make sense of the conflicting claims?

Chapter 3

What Are Some Alternatives to Banning Controversial Books?

This sculpture commemorates the 1933 mass burning of books by the Nazis. Many say that, in a free society, alternatives must be found to banning books simply because some do not agree with their content.

Editing the N-word Out of *Huckleberry Finn* Makes the Book Accessible to More Readers

"Teachers ... lamented the fact that they no longer felt justified in assigning either of Twain's boy books because of the hurtful n-word."

Alan Gribben

The following viewpoint was taken from a new edition of two novels by Mark Twain, titled *Mark Twain's Adventures of Tom Sawyer and Huckleberry Finn.* Editor Alan Gribben, who combined the two books into one volume, defends his much more controversial decision to replace some of Twain's original language with less offensive words—specifically, to replace the so-called n-word with the word "slave." *Huckleberry Finn* is a masterpiece of American literature, he notes, but many teachers are unwilling to teach it because of the offensive language. His editing, he argues, makes it possible for a great work of literature to be returned to the classroom.

Gribben is a professor of English at Auburn University, a noted Twain scholar, and a cofounder of the Mark Twain Circle of America.

AS YOU READ, CONSIDER THE FOLLOWING QUESTIONS:
1. How many times does the n-word appear in *Huckleberry Finn*, as reported by Gribben?
2. How long has the author been teaching *Tom Sawyer* and *Huckleberry Finn*?
3. How did Gribben decide which word to use in place of the n-word?

Far more controversial than this reuniting of Twain's boy books will be the editor's decision to eliminate two racial slurs[1] that have increasingly formed a barrier to these works for teachers, students, and general readers. The editor thus hopes to introduce both books to a wider readership than they can currently enjoy. Twain, it should be remembered, was endeavoring to accurately depict the prevailing social attitudes along the Mississippi River Valley during the 1840s by repeatedly employing in both novels a linguistic corruption of "Negro" in reference to African American slaves, and by tagging the villain in *Tom Sawyer* with a deprecating racial label for Native Americans. Although Twain's adult narrator of *Tom Sawyer* is himself careful to use the then-respectful terms "colored" and "negro" in Chapter 1, the boys refer to slaves four times with the pejorative n-word. In Twain's later book, *Huckleberry Finn*, these barely educated boys and the uneducated adult characters in Missouri and Arkansas casually toss about this same racial insult a total of 218 times (with the novel's table of contents adding another instance).

The n-word possessed, then as now, demeaning implications more vile than almost any insult that can be applied to other racial groups. There is no equivalent slur in the English language. As a result, with every passing decade this affront appears to gain rather than lose its impact. Even at the level of college and graduate school, students are capable of resenting textual encounters with this racial appellative. . . .

---

1. In addition to editing the n-word, Gribben changed the name "Injun Joe" to "Indian Joe."

The Editor's Story

Through a succession of firsthand experiences, this editor gradually concluded that an epithet-free edition of Twain's books is necessary today. For nearly forty years I have led college classes, bookstore forums, and library reading groups in detailed discussions of *Tom Sawyer* and *Huckleberry Finn* in California, Texas, New York, and Alabama, and I always refrained from uttering the racial slurs spoken by numerous characters, including Tom and Huck. I invariably substituted the word "slave" for Twain's ubiquitous n-word whenever I read any passages aloud. Students and audience members seemed to prefer this expedient, and I could detect a visible sense of relief each time, as though a nagging problem with the text had been addressed. Indeed, numerous communities currently ban *Huckleberry Finn* as required reading in public schools owing to its offensive racial language and have quietly moved the title to voluntary reading lists. The American Library Association lists the novel as one of the most frequently challenged books across the nation.

Over the years I have noted valiant and judicious defenses of the prevalence of the n-word in Twain's *Huckleberry Finn* as proposed by eminent writers, editors, and scholars, including those of Michael Patrick Hearn, Nat Hentoff, Randall Kennedy, and Jocelyn Chadwick-Joshua. Hearn, for example, correctly notes that "Huck says it out of habit, not malice." Apologists quite validly encourage readers to intuit the irony behind Huck's ignorance and to focus instead on Twain's larger satiric goals. Nonetheless, [poet] Langston Hughes made a forceful, lasting argument for omitting this incendiary word from all literature, however well-intentioned an author. "Ironically or seriously, of necessity for the sake of realism, or impishly for the sake of comedy, it doesn't matter," explained Hughes. African Americans, Hughes wrote, "do not like it in any book or play whatsoever, be the book or play ever so sympathetic. . . . They still do not like it."

Becoming a Problem

During the 1980s, educator John H. Wallace unleashed a fierce and protracted dispute by denouncing *Huckleberry Finn* as "the most grotesque example of racist trash ever written." In 1984 I had to walk past

Many groups agree that in Mark Twain's Huckleberry Finn, *the "n-word" should be replaced with "slave." The National Association for the Advancement of Colored People backed a student who opposed teaching the original book at a Washington high school.*

a picket line of African American parents outside a scholarly conference in Pennsylvania that was commemorating, among other achievements in American humor, the upcoming centenary anniversary of Twain's *Adventures of Huckleberry Finn.* James S. Leonard, then the editor of the newsletter for the Mark Twain Circle of America, conceded in 2001 that the racist language and unflattering stereotypes of slaves in *Huckleberry Finn* can constitute "real problems" in certain classroom settings. Another scholar, Jonathan Arac, has urged that students be prompted to read other, more unequivocally abolitionist works rather than this one novel that has been consecrated as the mandatory literary statement about American slavery. The once-incontestable belief that the reading of this book at multiple levels of schooling ought to be essential for every American citizen's education is cracking around the edges.

My personal turning point on the journey toward this present NewSouth Edition was a lecture tour I undertook in Alabama in 2009. I had written the introduction for an edition of *The Adventures of Tom Sawyer* designed to interest younger readers in older American literature. The volume was published by NewSouth Books for a consortium of Alabama libraries in connection with the "Big Read," an initiative sponsored by the National Endowment for the Arts. As I traveled around the state and spoke about the novel to reading groups of adults and teenagers in small towns like Valley, Dadeville, Prattville, Eufaula, Wetumpka, and Talladega, and in larger cities like Montgomery and Birmingham, I followed my customary habit of substituting the word "slave" when reading the characters' dialogue aloud. In several towns I was taken aside after my talk by earnest middle and high school teachers who lamented the fact that they no longer felt justified in assigning either of Twain's boy books because of the hurtful n-word. Here was further proof that this single debasing label is overwhelming every other consideration about *Tom Sawyer* and *Huckleberry Finn*, whereas what these novels have to offer readers hardly depends upon that one indefensible slur.

Word Exchanges

My understanding about this situation crystallized into a definite resolve. Unquestionably both novels can be enjoyed just as deeply and authentically if readers are not obliged to confront the n-word on so many pages. Consequently in this edition I have translated each usage of the n-word to read "slave" instead, since the term "slave" is closest in meaning and implication. Although the text loses some of the caustic sting that the n-word carries, that price seems small compared to the revolting effect that the more offensive word has on contemporary readers. Moreover, slavery is recognized globally as an affront to humanity.

I believe that a significant number of school teachers, college instructors, and general readers will welcome the option of an edition of Twain's fused novels that spares the reader from a racial slur that never seems to lose its vitriol. Despite occasional efforts of rap and hip hop musicians to appropriate the term, and well-meaning but usually futile (from my own experience) endeavors by classroom teachers to inoculate their students against it by using *Huckleberry*

American Library Association's Top Ten Most Frequently Challenged Books, 1990–1999

1. Scary Stories (series), by Alvin Schwartz

2. *Daddy's Roommate*, by Michael Willhoite

3. *I Know Why the Caged Bird Sings*, by Maya Angelou

4. *The Chocolate War*, by Robert Cormier

5. *The Adventures of Huckleberry Finn*, by Mark Twain

6. *Of Mice and Men*, by John Steinbeck

7. *Forever*, by Judy Blume

8. *Bridge to Terabithia*, by Katherine Paterson

9. *Heather Has Two Mommies*, by Lesléa Newman

10. *The Catcher in the Rye*, by J.D. Salinger

Finn as a springboard to discuss its etymology and cultural history, the n-word remains inarguably the most inflammatory word in the English language. The synonym "slave" expresses the cultural racism that Twain sought to convey, as in Huck Finn's report to Aunt Sally Phelps in Chapter 32 that a steamboat explosion had "killed a slave," to which she responds heartlessly, "Well, it's lucky; because sometimes people do get hurt."

EVALUATING THE AUTHOR'S ARGUMENTS:

In Viewpoint 4 of the previous chapter, author Susan Patron describes how the occurrence of one word appearing on one page caused her book *The Higher Power of Lucky* to be challenged and removed from several school libraries. In the viewpoint you have just read, by Alan Gribben, the controversy again centers on one word, but this time the word is used hundreds of times. What can you conclude from these cases? In your experience, does a shocking word gain or lose power when it is repeated? Would you have been affected by the presence of these words if no controversy had arisen around them? Why or why not?

Editing *Huckleberry Finn* Does a Disservice to Students

Charles E. May

In the following viewpoint, Charles E. May argues that editor Alan Gribben's decision to replace the n-word in Mark Twain's *Huckleberry Finn* with "slave" was a mistake. It is true, he agrees, that the character Huck comes from a racist culture and that he and other characters use offensive language. But Huck's rejection of his culture and appreciation for his friend Jim is the central conflict of the book, May argues, and cannot be represented in its full power without Twain's powerful language. He concludes that teachers should not shy away from teaching *Huckleberry Finn* as it was written.

May is a retired professor of English who taught at California State University–Long Beach and who writes the blog *Reading the Short Story*.

> *"If high-school teachers are afraid to teach a great work of literature, then we should change the teachers, not change the work."*

AS YOU READ, CONSIDER THE FOLLOWING QUESTIONS:
1. As suggested by the author, how much attention did Alan Gribben's new edition of *Huckleberry Finn* attract in newspapers?
2. What does Huckleberry Finn risk when he decides to protect his friend Jim from being captured, according to May?
3. As reported by the author, what play were the students of Monrovia High School not permitted to perform?

A ccording to various newspaper reports (and practically every newspaper in America, Ireland, England, and Canada has weighed in on this issue), Alan Gribben, chairman of the English department at Alabama's Auburn University, had become so frustrated teaching *Huckleberry Finn* because the word "nigger" is used over 200 times in it that he went to a small publisher, NewSouth, with the idea of replacing the word. Gribben told *Publishers Weekly*, "I was sought out by local teachers, and to a person, they said, 'We would love to teach . . . *Huckleberry Finn*, but we feel we can't do it anymore. In the new classroom, it's really not acceptable.'"

The founder of the press immediately saw she could sell a lot of copies with this idea, admitting that "if we can get [Twain's] book back into American schools, that would be really great for a small publishing company like ours." Honest enough. However, Gribben's justification for his decision is more than a little suspicious. He has said that Mark Twain was a notoriously commercial and populist author. "If he was alive today and all he had to do was change one word to get his book into every schoolhouse in America, he couldn't change it fast enough." That's pretty damned presumptuous, it seems to me.

Sweeping Debate Under the Rug

A few days ago, David Ulin of the *Los Angeles Times* (which is the paper I read every day) commented: "On its website, NewSouth notes that this new edition of *Huckleberry Finn* will not supersede previous editions of the novel: 'If the publication sparks good debate about how language impacts learning or about the nature of censorship or the way in which racial slurs exercise their baneful influence, then our mission in publishing this new edition of Twain's works will be more emphatically fulfilled,' the publisher declares.

"I don't know how that happens," Ulin declared, "how debate is stirred by sweeping what disturbs us under the rug. Gribben ought to understand this; it's supposed to be in the nature of his academic work. As for NewSouth, with its politically correct agenda, it might be useful to go back to Twain." It seems to me publicity and profit is more on NewSouth's agenda than political correctness.

Shown here is an original edition of Mark Twain's Adventures of Huckleberry Finn. *The author stresses that the main conflict confronting Huck is that his loyalty to the slave Jim flies in the face of his own religious and cultural heritage.*

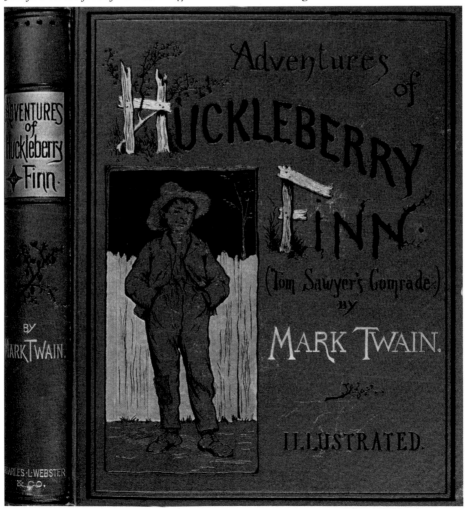

I grant you that "nigger" is a powerful word that refers to a shameful era in society's past, not just in America, but in other parts of the world. There is no way to justify the treatment of an entire race that the word reminds us of. And we should be reminded. However, it is not just that horrible treatment the word references, but the taboo nature of the utterance itself. . . .

I have taught *Huckleberry Finn* many times. Anyone who has read *Huckleberry Finn* knows that Huck's central conflict in the book is between his personal loyalty with Jim and his cultural and religious heritage that a slave is the property of his or her owner and that to protect Jim from being captured would not only mean he would be socially outcast himself, but that he would risk eternal damnation. In the most powerful scene in the book, Huck wrestles with this issue, but his friendship with Jim is more powerful than his cultural heritage, so in a declaration, the power of which must be understood in all its Bible Belt force, Huck decides in favor of the person rather than the policy and says: "All right, then, I'll go to hell."

Can Students Handle the Classics?

Tim Rutten in the *Los Angeles Times* this morning (January 8, 2011) called Professor Gribben's replacing the word "nigger" with the word "slave" and the word "Injun" in the name Injun Joe with "Indian" an "offensive idiocy of vandalism masquerading as sensitivity" and said it was one of those ideas "utterly breathtakingly off the mark."

FAST FACT

Translated into more than fifty languages, *Adventures of Huckleberry Finn* has sold more than 20 million copies worldwide.

Rutten then cited a Twain scholar, Judith Lee, who was this week quoted as saying she found nothing objectionable about the change, arguing that Twain's use of the term was meant to be read ironically, but that an appreciation of irony was an advanced interpretative skill, and that for a general audience a bowdlerized ["cleaned-up"] version would do just fine. To which Rutten rightly replied: "In

Do Not Edit *Huckleberry Finn*

In a 2011 Harris poll of 2,379 adults, whites were more likely than Hispanics or African Americans to say that the "n-word" should not be replaced with "slave" in *Huckleberry Finn*.

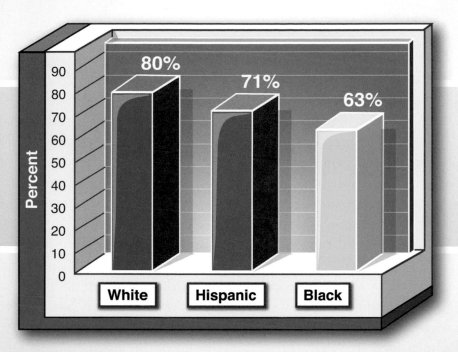

Taken from: Harris Interactive, press release, April 12, 2011.

other words, reserve the classics for sophisticated readers and give the masses Twain-lite. If you can't imagine what Mark Twain would make of that dichotomy, you've never read him."

Rutten also discussed a similar censorship issue at Monrovia High School, which has a highly regarded drama department, directed by a professional actor and teacher Marc Segal. This year Segal proposed the students put on Jonathan Larson's Pulitzer Prize–winning *Rent* as their spring musical. Last month, the school's principal asked to see the script and then consulted with the district's superintendent, after which she told Segal that *Rent* would have to be cancelled because: the play was not "family friendly" because it features "characters who have some dark issues they were dealing with." Rutten, of course, pointed out that such a criterion would eliminate just about every play from [Sophocles'] *Oedipus Rex* (incest) to [Shakespeare's] *Romeo and Juliet* (teenage sexuality). We can't have students reading literature that deals with "dark issues." Let them read about [bad-girl actress] Lindsay Lohan and watch reality TV.

The Humanities Under Pressure

In the kind of newspaper serendipity that I love, the *Los Angeles Times* also ran a story this morning on the current meeting of the Modern Language Association (MLA), the largest professional association of literature and foreign language teachers in the world (8000 in attendance this year). Rosemary Feal, executive director of the MLA, noted that the humanities are under greater pressure right now than they would be in economically better times. The problem may partly be the result of the misconception, she added, that English and foreign language studies do not prepare students for a range of careers, arguing that humanities are just as practical as any other major, especially during hard times when people need to be nimble about switching jobs. Well and good, but I agree with a Dartmouth American literature professor at the conference who argued that literature classes should not be justified only with arguments about student employability. "If you don't begin with the assumption that literature itself is a repository of human values that human beings need, then we lose everything." I would add to that, if we don't begin with the knowledge that reading literature is a powerful skill that enables us to see through the superficiality and silliness of much of modern culture, then, yes, we could lose everything. . . .

Good Literature Is Not Meant to Be an Easy Read

In my opinion, reading good literature is not easy, nor was it meant to be. Because literature is not life, but an artificial construct that makes use of language conventions to create some understanding of life, reading it carefully and correctly requires some training and knowledge of how language and literature work. To change a great work of literature because it makes some people uncomfortable is, of course, absurd. Literature should make people uncomfortable, and if high-school teachers are afraid to teach a great work of literature, then we should change the teachers, not change the work.

EVALUATING THE AUTHOR'S ARGUMENTS:

Both Charles E. May and Alan Gribben, who wrote the previous viewpoint, have had long careers as college professors, and both have taught *Huckleberry Finn* many times. What is it in their experiences, their tone, or their reasoning that helps you decide whose argument is more convincing?

Discussions of Evolution Should Be Flagged or Blacked Out from Science Textbooks

"Any theories about the origin of the universe are inherently religious."

Kent Hovind

In the following viewpoint, Kent Hovind argues against teaching evolution to high school science students; no one alive today witnessed the origins of life in the universe, he points out, so any claim that the theory of evolution is based in science is simply a lie. Because textbooks are required to be accurate, he continues, it is important to remove these false claims from the science books assigned in most classrooms. If new books cannot be purchased, he concludes, the false information should be cut out, blacked out, or pasted over, or schools should be required to inform students which information is false.

Hovind, a former high school math and science teacher, is the director of the Creation Science Evangelism ministry, dedicated to exposing evolution as a dangerous, religious worldview.

AS YOU READ, CONSIDER THE FOLLOWING QUESTIONS:
1. As defined in the viewpoint, what is the difference between education and indoctrination?
2. What three criteria must be met in order for something to be considered truly scientific, according to Hovind?
3. What kinds of stickers might districts place in science textbooks, as suggested by the author?

It has always amazed me how two different people can look at the same thing and reach two completely different conclusions. Two different people can look at the Grand Canyon. An evolutionist would say, "Wow, look what the Colorado River did over millions of years." The creationists would say, "Wow, look what the flood did in about thirty minutes!" Did it form slowly over millions of years? Or did it form rapidly during a giant flood like the one in the days of Noah described in the Bible?

Since no one saw it form, we must look at all the evidence and decide what to believe. If there are two or more ways of looking at something and you teach all possible theories, that is *education*. But if only one theory is taught, that is *indoctrination*.

There once was a farmer helping a cow with a breech birth, (the calf was coming out back feet first) when a city fellow happened by and saw the ordeal. The farmer was using a calf puller to try and remove the calf from the mother cow and he needed help. He asked the city fellow if he had ever seen anything like that. The city fellow said, "No." The farmer asked him if he had any questions. The city fellow said, "Yes. This has been bugging me for the last ten minutes. How fast do you think that calf was going when it ran into that cow?" No, no, no! They were not separating a wreck! Sometimes two people look at the same thing and one of them gets the wrong idea. The city fellow was looking at the situation all wrong.

Students today are only being shown one theory of the origin of the universe. Textbooks today contain many lies used to make the students believe in the evolution theory. The purpose of this booklet is to expose these lies in today's textbooks and present another more reasonable view of origins. . . .

What Should Be Taught in the Classroom?

The word science means "knowledge." Science is the study of what we know. In order for something to be truly scientific in the strict sense of the word, it must be *observable, testable, and demonstrable.* The entire subject of origins (both creation and evolution) is actually outside the field of science. No one alive today has observed the creation of the universe, and we cannot "do it again" in the laboratory to demonstrate how it happened. Nor is anyone alive who observed the "big bang" or the creation of life from non-living matter. *Any theories* about the origin of the universe are inherently religious (what we choose to trust, to believe in). . . .

FAST FACT

According to the most popular theory of creationism, the universe was created between 6,000 and 10,000 years ago, and the Great Flood occurred 1,656 years later.

Lies in the Textbook

Having taught high school science for 15 years, I will be quick to admit that there is much good science in most textbooks. However, there is some poison mixed in them. Did you know that rat poison is 99.99% good food? It is that .01% that is deadly. Please keep this in mind as you study your book; you will learn many facts from science that will help you for the rest of your life. I do not object to all the good things taught in science books, but I caution readers to be aware that most textbooks these days *are filled with their authors' philosophy of evolution.* . . .

What About False Information in Textbooks?

Most states have laws that require textbooks to be accurate. If your state does have such a law, see that it is enforced. If it does not, you may want to have this law passed. I believe it is only fair that false,

Opponents of textbooks about evolution recommend blacking out "offending" passages until such schoolbooks can be replaced.

outdated information be removed from the books. Until the time and money become available to replace the book, several options are available:

1. Have false information cut out or blacked out.
2. Have pages containing false information glued together.
3. Have stickers placed in the front of each book warning of false information by page number.
4. Require students be given a booklet detailing errors in their textbooks.

As a more long-term goal toward fixing the problem, students and parents alike should find out about how the textbooks are selected in your area and get involved in the process. Many school board members have not had the time to read all the books for themselves; they just go along with the recommendation of the committee reviewing the books. Students and parents can certainly get on the textbook selection committee or at least attend the meetings and voice their opinions and objections. If you are able to get on the textbook selection committee, select the least "poisonous" textbook. You could tell the other publishers why you didn't select their book (evolution

Four in Ten Americans Believe in Strict Creationism

In a 2010 Gallup poll, 40 percent of Americans expressed the opinion that "God created humans pretty much in their present form at one time within the last 10,000 years or so." The percentage has remained largely unchanged for three decades.

Which of the following statements comes closest to your views on the origin and development of human beings?

1) Human beings have developed over millions of years from less advanced forms of life, but God guided this process; 2) human beings have developed over millions of years from less advanced forms of life, but God had no part in this process; 3) God created human beings pretty much in their present form at one time within the last 10,000 years or so.

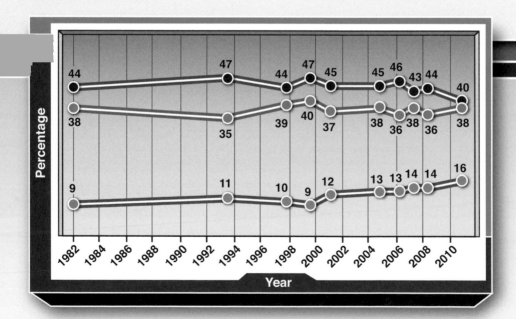

- ●= God created humans in present form
- ○= Humans evolved, with God guiding
- ○= Humans evolved, but God had no part in process

content). Then you could tell the publisher you chose why you chose them *this time*. Be sure to tell them if you find a textbook with less evolution in it next time, you will pick that one instead. Book publishers may also be willing to print a special, error-free version for your school district or state.

Do not confront your teacher publicly if it can be avoided. Try to talk to the teacher after class to share your concerns about the false information in the book. Most teachers are intelligent, sincere professionals who are only teaching what they have been taught. It may be that they have never seen the other side. Many teachers are creationists and would love to discuss the subject in class. Teachers may discuss Creation in science classes if they *wish*. You may find that your teacher is very supportive and would welcome the opportunity to discuss creation in class if a student brought it up. However, if you are late to class frequently, the class trouble-maker or goof off, never do your homework and *don't pay* attention in class, then please *don't* tell them you are a Christian!

Many students let their teachers watch my video series in class or allow other students to borrow them to watch at home. Scores of teachers have shown the series in their public school classrooms. This is perfectly fine and legal for them to do, even though some may be unnecessarily afraid of doing this.

If your teacher refuses to even consider the creation option, ask them to give me a call. I would be glad to answer any questions they have. Good educators educate students, they do not indoctrinate them with only one belief.

EVALUATING THE AUTHOR'S ARGUMENTS:

The viewpoint you have just read is unique among those in this book in being addressed to students, rather than to parents or educators. Examine the advice Kent Hovind gives students at the end of the viewpoint, guiding them in raising objections with their teachers. How does his tone in this section affect how you read the argument?

Viewpoint 4

Flagging Evolution Materials Inappropriately Promotes One Religion over Others

Austin Cline

"Science classes exist to teach students about science, not to indoctrinate them in a religious world view which they may not already share."

In the following viewpoint, Austin Cline argues against putting stickers, often called "disclaimers," in the fronts of science textbooks to warn that although the books may offer evolution as a fact, it is only a theory. These disclaimers, he contends, present false information themselves and wrongly imply that there is no scientific consensus about evolution. He concludes that disclaimers on science textbooks serve political or religious purposes that do not appropriately belong in public schools.

Cline is a writer who has written and lectured about atheism, agnosticism, and secular humanism for over fifteen years.

AS YOU READ, CONSIDER THE FOLLOWING QUESTIONS:
1. As reported by Cline, which state was the first, in 1998, to attempt to place disclaimers in science textbooks statewide?
2. What is the Cambrian Explosion, according to the disclaimer quoted by the author?
3. According to Cline, why are there no disclaimers proposed for geology or chemistry textbooks?

In recent years a popular tactic among creationists has been to get "disclaimers" put in school science texts. Because creationist efforts to have creationism taught alongside evolution have failed, they want to use disclaimers to cast doubt on the truth of evolution by telling students something like "evolution is only a theory." In fact, the close similarity of all these disclaimers is a sign that they are part of an organized effort by Evolution Deniers to undermine science in schools.

The first attempt to insert a disclaimer into science textbooks across an entire state occurred in Washington in 1998:

> This textbook discusses evolution, a controversial theory some scientists present as a scientific explanation for the origin of living things, such as plants, animals, and humans. No one was present when life first appeared on earth. Therefore, any statement about life's origins should be considered as theory, not fact.
>
> The word "evolution" may refer to many types of change. Evolution describes changes that occur within a species. (White moths, for example, may "evolve" into gray moths.) This process is microevolution, which can be observed and described as fact. Evolution may also refer to the change of one living thing to another, such as reptiles into birds. This process, called macroevolution, has never been observed and should be considered a theory. Evolution also refers to the unproven belief that random, undirected forces produced a world of living things.
>
> There are many unanswered questions about the origin of life which are not mentioned in your textbook, including: Why

did the major groups of animals suddenly appear in the fossil record (known as the "Cambrian Explosion")? Why have no new major groups of living things appeared in the fossil record for a long time? Why do major groups of plants and animals have no transitional forms in the fossil record? How did you and all living things come to possess such a complete and complex set of "Instructions" for building a living body?

Study hard and keep an open mind. Someday, you may contribute to the theories of how living things appeared on earth.

Evolution Disclaimers Misrepresent Science

It is true that no one was around when life first appeared, but evolution is not about the origins of life, it is about how life developed. This "mistake" is made exclusively by creationists trying to confuse and mislead people about evolution—when you see this sort of claim, you can be sure a creationist agenda is behind it. The same is true about presenting evolution as a theory rather than as a fact—evolution is both, but only creationists misrepresent this to people.

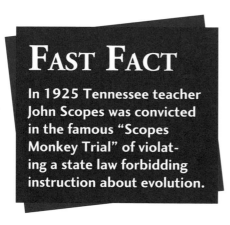

FAST FACT

In 1925 Tennessee teacher John Scopes was convicted in the famous "Scopes Monkey Trial" of violating a state law forbidding instruction about evolution.

It is not at all true that macroevolution (or speciation) has never been observed and is "only" a theory. Speciation has been observed in both the field and in the lab. Moreover, evolutionary biologists don't place a great deal of emphasis on the difference between microevolution and macroevolution because the line between the two is a feature of our perception of the world—there is no logical or biological barrier between them.

It is true that there are debates among scientists about some conceptual issues regarding how evolution can and does proceed; none of these debates, however, occur over whether or not evolution actually

"Children, this is your new science teacher."

"Children, this is your new science teacher," cartoon by Clive Goddard. www.CartoonStock.com. Copyright © by Clive Goddard. Reproduction rights obtainable from www.CartoonStock.com.

occurs, contrary to what the disclaimer implies. This is a common creationist tactic of misrepresenting genuine scientific disagreement over details as a nonexistent disagreement over general principles.

A Political Endorsement of Creationism

Little to none of the information contained in the disclaimers has any scientific basis. The disclaimers are not discussing or furthering science at all—if there were important scientific caveats about evolution which needed to be conveyed to students, they would be presented in the body of the text rather than on a sticker created by politicians.

Use of the disclaimer is a political rather than a scientific act, furthering political rather than scientific goals. The disclaimer is being used to communicate to students no less than five separate creationist myths, misunderstandings, and distortions about evolution. Creationists aren't able to get their message presented as part of the actual lesson plan, so they are using disclaimers to get around court rulings.

Shown here are biology textbooks being considered by the Texas State Board of Education for inclusion in schools. The teaching of evolution in science classes is a highly-charged political issue in the state.

Disclaimers Implicitly Misrepresent Science

Much of what is in evolution disclaimers could be written about many other aspects of science as well. No one was around when the earth and solar system formed. There are scientific debates over the meaning of quantum theory. Everything in science is supposed to proceed by tentative theories rather than dogmatic pronouncements.

Why aren't there additional disclaimers for geology, physics, chemistry, and other aspects of science? Why not have a general disclaimer emphasizing that science is always tentative? The answer is obvious: this isn't about science or education; instead, it's about powerful religious lobbying to have one aspect of science education weakened in order to pave the way for their religious beliefs to be taught in its place.

One implicit message in the disclaimers is that there is something "different" about evolution which requires it to get a special treatment or caveats. The truth is exactly the opposite, which means that students are being taught something fundamentally false about what science is and how science operates.

Why Disclaimers Are Wrong

Disclaimers represent a political and religious interference with scientific education. The government has an interest in determining what students learn in public schools, but no government body has the authority to force schools to teach falsehoods as part of a political and religious agenda.

Science classes exist to teach students about science, not to indoctrinate them in a religious world view which they may not already share. If parents disagree with science, they can teach their perspective at home and in their church; they should not, however, expect science education to be distorted and undermined to accommodate their dogmas.

EVALUATING THE AUTHOR'S ARGUMENTS:

In the viewpoint you have just read, Austin Cline charges that the disclaimer from the state of Washington in school science books includes "no less than five separate creationist myths, misunderstandings, and distortions about evolution"; however, he does not list or refute them. Are the five things he refers to easy to identify? How does his decision not to develop this claim in more detail affect your reading of the argument?

Parents Should Help Kids Find Alternatives to Inappropriate Readings

Betty Holcomb

"Not only can you say [no], but you should."

In the following viewpoint, journalist Betty Holcomb argues that the best way to handle a child's desire to read something inappropriate is often for the parent to simply say "no." Many children have reading levels beyond their maturity levels, she points out, and parents need to keep the lines of communication open to find out what their children are reading and are interested in reading. If parents are prepared with good questions and appealing alternative titles, she concludes, they can keep their advanced readers happy and safe.

Holcomb is policy director for the Center for Children's Initiatives, a nonprofit organization that works to improve early education across New York State. She has written widely on work and family issues for the national media.

AS YOU READ, CONSIDER THE FOLLOWING QUESTIONS:

1. In what way do many parents wish bookstores and libraries were like movie theaters, as explained by Holcomb?
2. Where can parents go to learn about the reading levels of books their children are interested in, according to the author?
3. As reported by Holcomb, what is likely to be a child's reaction if a parent suggests reading a book along with the child?

You've spent years nurturing your child's love of reading, starting with those delicious early days on your lap, patting the bunny. These days, he's reading well above grade level, savoring the adventures of Harry Potter and *The Hobbit*. He's now able to read just about anything, and that's been a source of unqualified pride and delight for both of you.

Until the day your 11 year old tells you he's heard Stephen King's *Bag of Bones* is the greatest book. You know it's way too mature for him, will scare him out of his wits, and keep both of you up for nights to come. Or until the time your 12-year-old daughter insists that Danielle Steele is just the *best* author, the babysitter told her so. At these moments, you are asking yourself why the library, the bookstore, or at least the school library doesn't have one of those rating systems for books the way theaters do for movies. A simple "R" on the cover would let you off the hook. How do you say "no" to a book after all those years of insisting that reading was the most valuable skill he'd ever acquire?

> ## FAST FACT
>
> The Newbery Medal, recognizing a distinguished contribution to literature for children, has been awarded every year since 1922. The Printz Award, for excellence in young adult literature, was first awarded in 2000.

Not to worry. Not only can you say it, but you should. "Not every book is for every child," says Pat Scales, author of *Teaching Banned Books* and a middle-school librarian for 28 years. "It is perfectly okay to say 'no' to some books."

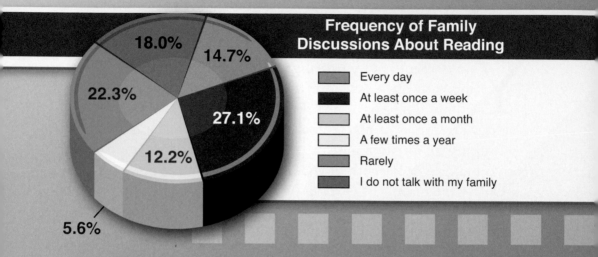

Family Discussions of Reading

A 2009 survey of more than 17,000 British students aged eight to sixteen showed that most students have discussions with their families about what they are reading, at least occasionally.

Frequency of Family Discussions About Reading

18.0%
14.7%
22.3%
27.1%
12.2%
5.6%

- Every day
- At least once a week
- At least once a month
- A few times a year
- Rarely
- I do not talk with my family

Taken from: National Literacy Trust, *Literacy in the Home and Young People's Reading*, executive summary, 2010.

Even necessary, she insists, when you have a prepubescent advanced reader on your hands. "One of the biggest mistakes I see both parents and teachers making is thinking that gifted children or avid readers can handle anything. They can't," says Scales. "Some of the most gifted readers are the most immature children I have ever met."

So that's the why. What about the how? "Keep it positive, keep the conversation going and offer other, better options," says Larra Clark, a spokeswoman for the American Library Association.

Easy for her to say—she doesn't know your child. How do you make "no" into a positive statement? How do you deflect the arguments of your very advanced reader—who also happens to be a very advanced debater? In fact, you're pretty certain he'll turn into a champion defender of the First Amendment the moment he senses you don't like his choice.

Try these strategies:

- Accentuate the positive. "I would never say 'no' exactly," says Scales. "That can turn the book into forbidden treasure. I'd say, 'That's a good book, but knowing you, you'd like this other one better.'" That tactic raises your child's curiosity, redirects his focus, and also shows how much you care about him. "There's not a kid in the world—or an adult for that matter—who doesn't feel good when told that someone, especially a parent, is thinking about him and what he likes," says Scales.
- Zero in on what he likes. Figuring that out is both easier and harder than it sounds. It's not always the author or the overall subject. "More often than not, it's the emotional content that captures kids, and parents sometimes miss that," Scales says. "He may like a book about the Revolutionary War, for example, not because it's about war, but because the story is really about the relationship between two brothers. Once you identify the emotional hook, you can find other books about that issue."
- Check out the books. Check out reviews, book covers, and publishers' Web sites for information on reading levels, as well as the age level for the content and see our advice on choosing books. The reading level cues you in to the vocabulary and language issues; the age level gives you the experts' rating on how old kids should be before they tackle the content. Be on the lookout for certain prizes and awards—the Newbery Award, for example, guarantees a consensus among experts that these books are terrific choices for any child up to the age of 13, and the Printz Award covers top young-adult choices. For more suggestions, see our collection of booklists.
- Know the authors. Once your child finds a favorite author, she'll probably want to read every volume that writer ever penned. That makes the search for new books easier for a time, but keep a watchful eye on the titles he chooses. Some writers cross over into adult material. Elementary-school favorite Judy Blume, for example, also wrote *Wifey*, definitely adult material. Author Carl Hiaasen published *Hoot*, a hit with the 9- to 12-year-old set, but his other books, from *Strip Tease* to *Basket Case*, are adults-only fare.

The author says that parents should monitor the books their kids are reading, as well as the authors—who may write books for both kids and adults.

- Offer to share. When your child insists on reading something that gives you the willies, consider this sneaky, but often effective tactic. "Tell your child that you've been wanting to read that book, and so why don't you do it together?" says Scales. "Most often, that will be a turn-off, and she'll move on to something else."

What if she doesn't? What if she still wants to read *Wifey* or Stephen King? Then there are only two choices left. "You always have the right to set limits and simply say, 'I'm sorry, but I don't want you reading that book at your age,'" says Scales. Or, she suggests, treat it as one of those rare opportunities to explore values and issues that you didn't know, up until this very moment, your child was ready for. "In the end, I have great confidence in children," says Scales. "They often know what they are ready for, even though you didn't recognize it yourself yet. When that happens, I suggest to parents that they do read it together, talk about the issues together, and grow together. That can be the most surprising and best experience of all."

EVALUATING THE AUTHOR'S ARGUMENTS:

The viewpoint you have just read by Betty Holcomb is written by a parent, for parents to read, but it describes, in effect, how to convince children into changing their minds about books they want to read. Which of the strategies suggested in the viewpoint do you think would be most successful? Which strategies would not lead to the desired effect in your opinion? Why?

Facts About Banned Books

Editor's note: These facts can be used in reports to add credibility when making important points or claims.

Challenged and Banned Books

According to the American Library Association's Office for Intellectual Freedom, the ten most frequently challenged books of the decade from 2000 through 2009 were:
- Harry Potter series, by J.K. Rowling
- Alice series, by Phyllis Reynolds Naylor
- *The Chocolate War,* by Robert Cormier
- *And Tango Makes Three,* by Justin Richardson and Peter Parnell
- *Of Mice and Men,* by John Steinbeck
- *I Know Why the Caged Bird Sings,* by Maya Angelou
- Scary Stories series, by Alvin Schwartz
- His Dark Materials series, by Philip Pullman
- ttyl, ttfn, and l8r, g8r series, by Lauren Myracle
- *The Perks of Being a Wallflower,* by Stephen Chbosky

The American Library Association's lists of the Top 100 Banned/ Challenged Books of 2000 through 2009 and 1990 through 1999 include several picture books for children; for example:
- *Daddy's Roommate,* by Michael Willhoite
- *Draw Me a Star,* by Eric Carle
- *Heather Has Two Mommies,* by Lesléa Newman
- *In the Night Kitchen,* by Maurice Sendak
- *King & King,* by Linda de Haan
- *And Tango Makes Three,* by Justin Richardson and Peter Parnell
- *Where's Waldo?* by Martin Hanford

The American Library Association's database keeps track of the kinds of institutions whose materials are challenged. According to the database, for the years 1990–2010:

- K–12 schools faced 4,048 challenges; colleges and universities faced 151.
- K–12 school libraries faced 3,659 challenges; public libraries faced 2,679; college libraries faced 62.

Public Opinions of Book Banning

According to a Harris poll conducted in March 2011 that surveyed adults about book banning:
- Fifty-six percent said that books should never be banned completely, while 18 percent said that some books should be banned, and 26 percent were not at all sure.
- According to 83 percent of the respondents, school libraries should make copies of the Holy Bible available to children; 59 percent believe that school libraries should have the Jewish Torah or Talmud; 57 percent believe that school libraries should have the Muslim Koran (also spelled *Quran*).
- Seventy-six percent said that books discussing evolution should be available in school libraries; 57 percent said books about vampires should be available; 52 percent favor the availability of books about drugs or alcohol; 50 percent favor availability of books about witchcraft or sorcery.
- Most Americans—62 percent—said that school libraries should not carry books with explicit language.
- Adults were almost evenly divided over books with references to sex: 48 percent said they should be available, while 45 percent said they should not be.

In April and May 2005, a Gallup youth survey asked teens aged thirteen to seventeen about what their schools can and should censor. The results were as follows:
- Fifty-six percent said that it is not appropriate for school officials to ban books, newspapers, or magazines that they consider offensive; 44 percent said it is appropriate.
- Teens aged thirteen to fifteen were more likely than those aged sixteen or seventeen to find the restrictions appropriate.

Sacred Books and Book Banning

- In June 2011, members of Pakistan's parliament called for the Bible, the holy book of Christians, to be banned in accordance with Pakistan's laws against blasphemy.
- In June 2010, Pastor Terry Jones announced that he would hold a public "Burn a Quran Day," burning two hundred copies of the Muslim holy book. After an international outcry, he canceled the event, but one of his followers burned a copy at Jones's Florida church in March 2011.
- In October 2009, the Amazing Grace Baptist Church of Canton, North Carolina, which accepts only the King James Version of the Bible as the Word of God, destroyed copies of other translations.
- In May 2008, several copies of the Christian New Testament were burned in the city of Or Yehuda, Israel.
- In August 2007, Dutch politician Geert Wilders called for the Koran, the holy book of Muslims, to be banned in the Netherlands.
- In the 1930s and 1940s, Nazis held several public book burnings in Germany during which they destroyed copies of the Jewish Torah as well as copies of the Jehovah's Witness version of the Bible and the sacred texts of Muslims and Zoroastrians.

Organizations to Contact

The editors have compiled the following list of organizations concerned with the issues debated in this book. The descriptions are derived from materials provided by the organizations. All have publications or information available for interested readers. The list was compiled on the date of publication of the present volume; the information provided here may change. Be aware that many organizations take several weeks or longer to respond to inquiries, so allow as much time as possible for the receipt of requested materials.

American Booksellers Foundation for Free Expression (ABFFE)
19 Fulton St., Ste. 407, New York, NY 10038
(212) 587-4025 • fax: (212) 587-2436
website: www.abffe.com

The mission of the ABFFE, the bookseller's voice in the fight against censorship, is to promote and protect the free exchange of ideas, particularly those contained in books, by opposing restrictions on the freedom of speech; issuing statements on significant free expression controversies; participating in legal cases involving First Amendment rights; collaborating with other groups with an interest in free speech; and providing education about the importance of free expression. With the National Council Against Censorship, the ABFFE sponsors the Kids Right to Read project. Online resources include a *Banned Books Handbook,* the "ABFFE Update," and information about books for sale.

American Center for Law and Justice (ACLJ)
PO Box 90555, Washington, DC 20090-0555
(800) 296-4529
website: www.aclj.org
The ACLJ focuses on constitutional law, specifically the ideal that religious freedom and freedom of speech are inalienable, God-given rights. The organization has participated in numerous cases regarding student education rights and the freedom of parents to make decisions

about their children's education, believing that parents should have the right to opt their children out of classes and course materials that conflict with the parents' religious convictions. Its website provides radio and television feeds, podcasts, photos, news releases, and commentaries, as well as petitions and online forms for generating letters to editors and elected officials.

American Civil Liberties Union (ACLU)
125 Broad St., 18th Fl., New York, NY 10004
website: www.aclu.org
Founded in 1920, the ACLU is a nonprofit and nonpartisan organization of more than five hundred thousand members and supporters. The mission of the ACLU is to preserve all of the protections and guarantees of the US Constitution's Bill of Rights. The group handles nearly six thousand court cases annually from offices in almost every state. Its website has a collection of news articles, as well as a blog, newsfeeds, podcasts, and "Stand Up with the ACLU," a section dedicated to youth issues. Publications include legal and legislative facts sheets and reports, as well as articles about banned books and Banned Books Week.

American Library Association (ALA)
50 E. Huron St., Chicago, IL 60611
(800) 545-2433
website: www.ala.org
Founded in 1876, the ALA provides leadership for the development, promotion, and improvement of library and information services and the profession of librarianship in order to enhance learning and ensure access to information for all. The ALA's Office for Intellectual Freedom collects information about books that are banned or challenged in libraries and schools, supports librarians who are facing demands to restrict materials, publishes lists of frequently challenged books by year and by decade, and cosponsors an annual Banned Books Week to promote the freedom to read.

Censor the Book
PO Box 177907, Dallas, TX 75201
e-mail: censorthebook@gmail.com
website: www.freewebs.com/censorthebook

Censor the Book is an organization dedicated to the banning or censoring of books that it considers indecent, immoral, racist, and unfit for society. Sponsored by Christian organizations and concerned groups that promote "antidefamation" in literature and entertainment, it seeks to stop the availability of these kind of books in schools, libraries, and retail stores. Its website includes a long list of sponsoring organizations, lists of the most-censored books for individual years, pages dedicated to "Bad Books" and "Bad Authors," and a collection of news articles about efforts to ban books.

Family Research Council (FRC)
801 G St. NW, Washington, DC 20001
(800) 225-4008
website: www.frc.org

Since 1983, the FRC has advanced faith, family, and freedom in public policy and public opinion through policy research, public education on Capitol Hill and in the media, and grassroots mobilization. Believing that God is the author of life, liberty, and the family, FRC promotes the Judeo-Christian worldview as the basis for a just, free, and stable society. The website has blogs, e-mail subscriptions, legal documents, and reports on a wide range of conservative issues. Its materials pertaining to the issue of banned books include a brochure titled "Homosexuality in Your Child's School" and the report "Who Should Decide How Children Are Educated."

Gateways to Better Education
PO Box 514, Lake Forest, CA 92609-0514
(949) 586-5437 • fax: (949) 457-6361
e-mail: info@gtbe.org • website: www.gtbe.org

Gateways to Better Education is a nonprofit organization founded in 1991 to help public schools teach about the important contribution it believes the Bible and Christianity make to the world. It produces articles for parents and teachers, lesson plan ideas, professional development seminars for teachers, parenting workshops, and print and online materials. Its web articles include "When to Remove Your Child from an Activity," "Challenging a Book in Your School," and "By the Book: Understanding the Proper Process for Removing a Book."

National Coalition Against Censorship (NCAC)
275 Seventh Ave., #1504, New York, NY 10001
(212) 807-6222 • fax: (212) 807-6245
e-mail: ncac@ncac.org • website: www.ncac.org

The NCAC, founded in 1974, is an alliance of fifty national literary, artistic, religious, educational, professional, labor, and civil liberties groups. NCAC works to educate the public about the dangers of censorship and how to oppose it. It sponsors the Youth Free Expression Network (YFEN), which provides speakers and films. Its website includes a resource guide, "Censorship in Schools: Learning, Speaking, and Thinking Freely; The First Amendment in Schools," and a Banned Books Toolkit.

National Council of Teachers of English (NCTE)
1111 W. Kenyon Rd., Urbana, IL 61801-1096
(877) 369-6283
website: www.ncte.org

The NCTE, founded in 1911, is devoted to improving the teaching and learning of English and the language arts at all levels of education. Through its Anti-Censorship Center it offers advice, helpful documents, and other support at no cost to teachers faced with challenges to literary works, films and videos, drama productions, or teaching methods. Reports and pages available on the NCTE website include "Students' Right to Read," "Rationales for Teaching Challenged Books," and "Guidelines for Selection of Materials in English Language Arts Programs."

Parents and Students for Academic Freedom (K–12)
Attn: Sara Dogan
Students for Academic Freedom
4401 Wilshire Blvd., 4th Fl., Los Angeles, CA 90010
(888) 527-3321
e-mail: sara@studentsforacademicfreedom.org
website: www.psaf.org

Parents and Students for Academic Freedom (K–12) is a subgroup of the college-focused Students for Academic Freedom. The organization's mission is to counter what it sees as inappropriate left-wing or politically correct influences on public education. Its website offers news, commentary, e-mail updates and newsletters, and an Academic Freedom Code. Articles include "Agenda Pushing and Censorship in Secondary Schools" and "How I Changed My Left-Wing High School."

People for the American Way
2000 M St. NW, Ste. 400, Washington, DC 20036
(800) 326-7329
e-mail: pfaw@pfaw.org • website: www.pfaw.org

People for the American Way was founded in 1981 to meet the challenges of discord and fragmentation by calling on the values of pluralism; individuality; freedom of thought, expression, and religion; a sense of community; and tolerance and compassion for others. Its website offers newsletters, press releases, action items, a clickable map so readers can track issues in their own states, and reports including "Parental Rights: The Trojan Horse of the Religious Right's Attack on Public Education" and "What You Can Do to Protect Public Education!"

SafeLibraries
641 Shunpike Rd., #123, Chatham, NJ 07928
e-mail: safelibraries@gmail.com • website: www.safelibraries.org

SafeLibraries is dedicated to protecting children and families from what it believes are the dangerous policies of the American Library Association (ALA). Specifically, SafeLibraries opposes many of the ALA's recommendations about the age-appropriateness of individual books, its positions on censorship, and its resistance to Internet filtering in public libraries. The organization's website offers a blog, videos from local and national news programs, and links to other organizations and reports.

For Further Reading

Books

Boyer, Paul S. *Purity in Print: Book Censorship in America from the Gilded Age to the Computer Age.* 2nd ed. Madison: University of Wisconsin Press, 2002. A cultural historian traces the shifting tides of censorship through American history since the Civil War, enriching the narrative with illustrations, interviews, and excerpts from court cases.

Carefoote, Pearce J. *Forbidden Fruit: Banned, Censored, and Challenged Books from Dante to Harry Potter.* Toronto: LMB Editions, 2007. Carefoote, a theology professor and librarian, gives an overview of the reasons books are challenged or banned and argues for the freedom to read, focusing on censorship in Canada.

Doyle, Robert P. *Banned Books: Challenging Our Freedom to Read.* Chicago: American Library Association, 2010. The American Library Association issues new editions of this project every few years. This 2010 edition includes a general discussion of the freedom to read, ideas for celebrating Banned Books Week, and brief analyses of dozens of challenged or banned books with court cases and quotations from major figures.

Foerstel, Herbert N. *Banned in the USA: A Reference Guide to Book Censorship in Schools and Public Libraries.* Rev. ed. Charlotte, NC: IAP, 2006. In four parts, this book surveys major incidents of banning, the laws regarding book censorship, interviews with authors whose works have been challenged, and a list of the most frequently censored books of the 1990s.

Green, Jonathon. *The Encyclopedia of Censorship.* Rev. ed. by Nicholas Karolides. New York: Facts On File, 2005. This large volume is an alphabetical collection of articles on the major books, films, authors, themes, and organizations involved in censorship in the United States and in other countries.

Harrison, Maureen, and Steve Gilbert. *Obscenity and Pornography Decisions of the United States Supreme Court.* Carlsbad, CA:

Excellent Books, 2000. This volume collects fourteen important United States Supreme Court decisions, edited into accessible English for general readers.

MacDonald, Joan Vos. *J.K. Rowling: Banned, Challenged, and Censored.* Berkeley Heights, NJ: Enslow, 2008. This discussion of the Harry Potter series as it has faced challenges in the United States and Europe gives a fair treatment to all sides of the controversy and includes discussion questions for students.

Scales, Pat. *Teaching Banned Books: 12 Guides for Young Readers.* Chicago: American Library Association, 2001. A well-known expert on children's literature presents discussion guides for twelve frequently challenged books, including *The Giver, My Brother Sam Is Dead,* and *Roll of Thunder, Hear My Cry*, showing how teachers can use these books in the classroom while respecting different views.

Singham, Mano. *God vs. Darwin: The War between Evolution and Creationism in the Classroom.* Lanham, MD: Rowman & Littlefield Education, 2009. Mano, a scientist, presents a history of eighty years of legal battles over whether the teaching of evolution belongs in the classroom.

Thomas, R. Murray. *What Schools Ban and Why.* Westport, CT: Praeger, 2008. This evenhanded book looks at various things that public schools attempt to restrict—from books to cell phones to T-shirts.

Wartzman, Rick. *Obscene in the Extreme: The Burning and Banning of John Steinbeck's "The Grapes of Wrath."* New York: PublicAffairs, 2008. This book focuses on the reception in California of Steinbeck's Pulitzer Prize–winning novel. In 1939, the book was banned in one California county, in part because of the perceived offensiveness of the language and for sexual situations, but mostly because of the novel's depictions of farm owners.

Periodicals

Bilyeu, Suzanne. "Mark Twain's Bad Boy," *New York Times Upfront,* March 1, 2010.

Boston, Rob. "Fanning the Flames: The 'Golden Age' of American Book Burning," *Humanist,* July/August 2008.

Bucher, Katherine T., and M. Lee Manning. "Intellectual Freedom for Young Adolescents," *Childhood Education*, September 22, 2007.

DeMitchell, Todd A., and John J. Carney. "Harry Potter and the School Library," *Phi Delta Kappan*, October 2005.

Galehouse, Maggie. "Not for Our Kids?," *Houston Chronicle*, September 22, 2010.

Gallo, Don. "Censorship, Clear Thinking, and Bold Books for Teens," *English Journal*, January 2008.

Glanzer, Perry L. "Harry Potter's Provocative Moral World: Is There a Place for Good and Evil in Moral Education?," *Phi Delta Kappan*, March 2008.

Gurdon, Meghan Cox. "Darkness Too Visible," *Wall Street Journal*, June 4, 2011.

Imrich, Barbara. "What's in a Word?," *Knowledge Quest*, November/December 2007.

Kauer, Suzanne M. "A Battle Reconsidered: Second Thoughts on Book Censorship and Conservative Parents," *English Journal*, January 2008.

Lewis, Harry. "Not Your Father's Censorship," *Chronicle of Higher Education*, January 16, 2009.

Martinson, David L. "Responding Intelligently to Would-Be Censors," *Education Digest*, September 2007.

Muncy, Mitchell. "Finding Censorship Where There Is None," *Wall Street Journal*, September 25, 2009.

O'Connor, Barbara. "Keeping It Real: How Realistic Does Realistic Fiction for Children Need to Be?," *Language Arts*, July 2010.

Richey, Warren. "Supreme Court: Miami School Can Ban Book on Cuba," *Christian Science Monitor*, November 16, 2009.

Scales, Pat. "What Makes a Good Banned Book?," *Horn Book Magazine*, September/October 2009.

Scales, Pat. "When Weeding Is Wrong: A Principal Asks for Banned Books to Be Removed from the Collection," *School Library Journal*, November 2009.

Sennitt, Jo. "Banned Books and Intellectual Freedom," *School Librarian*, Summer 2009.

Tang, Didi, and Mary Beth Marklein. "Those Challenging Books Find Strength in Numbers," *USA Today*, December 1, 2010.

Walters, Hetert-Qebu. "Educate, Don't Censor: *The Adventures of Huckleberry Finn* and the N-word," *Huffington Post*, January 12, 2011.

Wu, Tim. "The Future of Free Speech," *Chronicle of Higher Education*, November 19, 2010.

Websites

Banned Books Online (http://digital.library.upenn.edu/books/banned-books.html). A narrative list of books that have been challenged or banned, with dozens of links to further information about specific books and cases.

Beacon for Freedom of Expression (www.beaconforfreedom.org). An international database of more than fifty thousand titles, including censored works and books and articles about censorship and the freedom of expression.

Parents Against Bad Books in Schools (www.pabbis.com). A list of dozens of books offered in kindergarten through twelfth-grade curricula and libraries, with excerpts showing why they are controversial and might not be appropriate for children.

Plan2Succeed (www.plan2succeed.org). A negative review of American Library Association policies on pornography and Internet filtering, with quotations from parents and excerpts from relevant court decisions.

Index

Picture Credits

© Bill Adams/Express-Times/Landov, 37

© AFP/Getty Images, 95

© AP Images/Harry Cabluck, 102

© AP Images/The Gadsden Times, Marc Golden, 10

© AP Images/Chitose Suzuki, 45

© AP Images/Ted S. Warren, 81

© AP Images/Dale Wetzel, 70

© [apply pictures]/Alamy, 108

© Duffy-Marie Arnoult/Wire Image/Getty Images, 74

© Brad Barket/Getty Images, 39

© EPA/Mike Nelson/Landov, 49

Gale/Cengage Learning, 15, 24, 34, 42, 50, 65, 69, 83, 89, 96, 106

© Jacob Langston/Orlando Sentinel/MCT via Getty Images, 29

© Evy Mages/Washington Post/Getty Images, 22

© Stapleton Collection/Corbis, 87

© Andrew Taylor/Alamy, 13

© Justine Walker/Alamy, 77